Richard M. Sharp

THE FOUR CUPS OF BETROTHAL

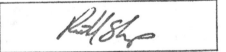

GlobalEdAdvance
Press

DEDICATION

This book is dedicated to

JASON MILLER AND THAD WILHOIT

Thank you for the joy each of you have brought into my life. I thank God upon every remembrance of the moments in which each of you asked for the hand of my daughters. I am a blessed man for the arrangement and I have never regretted it. I pray that your children will grow to embrace the rich traditions that come to us from the scriptures and to cherish the Jewish roots of our faith. My desire is that they will themselves be betrothed to Jesus by making Him their Lord and choose to serve Him faithfully all their days.

I hope to live to see your sons one day ask a God-fearing man for the hand of his daughter. I will consider my life a success if my grandchildren grow to love Israel and choose to stand in solidarity with her. What they see in your home will make the difference. A blessing on your house!

PUBLISHER'S NOTE

"Further up and further in..."

This book is the result of years of research tracking the steps in betrothal and marriage. Much time was spent in historic libraries searching for data on the issue. As C.S. Lewis once shared, *"Further up and further in..."* you will find true facts.

This is what Dr. Sharp did for many years tracing the Jewish roots of Christianity in the ancient writings. The language, translation and spelling of proper names and places are as he found them in the ancient books and influenced by Strong (1890). The NIV in Jeremiah 6:16 speaks to the process at hand: *This is what the LORD says: "Stand at the crossroads and look; ask for the ancient paths, ask where the good way is, and walk in it, and you will find rest for your souls..."*

CONTENTS

FOREWORD

King David had his mighty men of valor. My brother, Dr. Rick Sharp, was one of God's mighty men of valor! He was a man with a message and God took him to the nations. How GREAT is our God! May He continue to bless and give increase to the ministry to which Rick was called.

Through prayer and decades of study on the Jewish roots of the Christian faith, God gave him great insight into our betrothal to the LORD. As you read this book, may you gain a deeper appreciation of our redemption and union with the LORD. May you hear God speak to you as I did.

Though I miss him terribly, he is where he belongs. He is with the Ancient of Days always beholding the glory of God!

Philip Sharp

AUTHOR'S PREFACE

"Will you go with this man?"

There were a total of four cups of wine in the ritual of betrothal and marriage: Sanctification, Salvation, Redemption, and Deliverance. In the betrothal act, men came to ask for the hand of a daughter of the house. It was not a common event for the household; it was special, set apart as unique, and considered a holy act with significant repercussions. In the Middle Ages the two ceremonies were combined into one, but in the Biblical period the two ceremonies were distinct.

On the occasion of the betrothal, the first cup was filled with wine and drank as a toast to set apart the occasion as something significant. Each of the feasts of Israel, every Sabbath, and special life events in Judaism all begin with a cup of wine and a blessing sanctifying the event. This act is known as קידוש – *Kiddush*, which literally means "sanctification."

In the ancient betrothal ritual, after the cup of sanctification was partaken, the second cup would be filled with wine, but not immediately imbibed. It was now time for the father of the bride-to-be to elaborate about his daughter. He would speak about the character of his daughter, her talents, and skills. He would speak in detail about her chores around the house and how her absence would bring him great distress. The father of the bride-to-be was establishing a level of worth from which he would negotiate a price for his daughter.

In the ancient betrothal rite, a third cup would be filled
with wine and once the Ketubah was read aloud, which is the
marriage contract that included the *Tenaim conditions,* the
groom-to-be would drink from the cup. The bride-to-be would
then be asked the same question that Rebecca had been
asked, namely, *wilt thou go with this man* (Genesis 24:58).
If she said yes, she would then drink from the same cup of
wine. The agreement having been toasted, the vessel was
then broken to signify that, *just as a broken vessel can never
be repaired, so is a broken engagement irreparable* (Goldin,
1956).

Jesus had promised His disciples in the Upper Room
that He would not drink the fruit of the vine until *the kingdom
of God shall come* (Luke 22:18). He fulfilled this purpose,
paid the prescribed bride price, and had betrothed Himself
with His action. His disciples were now in the world, but
not of it (John 17:15). Their identity had changed, and He
assured them that they had not chosen Him, but that He
had chosen them. Their sin debt had been transferred to
their beloved; they would now enjoy His inheritance. He
pronounced them ceremonially clean through the word
spoken to them (John 15:3). In His absence, their needs
would be met by His Father and all they had to do was ask in
His name. He had given the gift of another Comforter (Holy
Spirit) and had promised that He was going to prepare a
place for them and would return.

The meta-narrative of betrothal had been embedded
within the events related in the Gospels. Only the fourth cup
has been left untouched. Betrothal has occurred for all who
have embraced Jesus. The actual marriage is yet to come.

Christianity has commemorated Jesus' discourse in
the Upper Room as the initiation of a *new covenant* replete

with a new ordinance called Holy Communion or the Eucharist. The Apostle Paul, when writing to the Corinthian church, gave great insight into this ordinance. What was the meaning behind the expression, *as oft as ye drink it* (I Corinthians 11:25)? Paul certainly had no denominational or ecclesiastical bias that he was trying to address with the Gentile Corinthian believers three decades after Jesus had died. Jesus had been celebrating a Passover *Seder* meal with His disciples when the ordinance was instituted. It is a plausible argument that the expression, *as oft as ye drink it* referred to the annual Passover *Seder* or Pesach. No longer would the disciples commemorate Pesach as a remembrance of being set free from bondage to Egypt; now they would commemorate it as a celebration of freedom from the bondage to sin. *This do in remembrance of me* links the celebration to Jesus' selfless action on the cross.

The time for the marriage nuptials between Jesus and His bride is uncertain but already determined. The meta-narrative of betrothal suggests it and John's revelation described it. When it actually does occur, it will not be a surprise for Jesus and His bride to drink from the fourth cup, after which Jesus will lay the cup on the earth and crush it with His foot. Nothing and no one to ever come between the covenant of marriage established as betrothal on the cross.

Dr. Sharp teaching *The Four Cups of Betrothal*

CHAPTER ONE

THE META-NARRATIVE OF BETROTHAL

This work will examine how the ritual of betrothal has framed the meta-narrative of God's relationship with man. This suggests that a formal wedding between God and man is in the offing, and that the legal marriage has already occurred through the act of betrothal. This ritual of betrothal is suggested by scriptural texts from Genesis to Revelation. The author has understood the term "ritual" to be akin to Zuesse's definition; namely, *those conscious and voluntary, repetitious and stylized symbolic bodily actions that are centered on cosmic structure and/or sacred presence* (Zeusse, 1987, p. 405).

Jean Francois Lyotard coined the expression "meta-narrative" in his 1979 work entitled, *The Post-Modern Condition: A Report on Knowledge.* He was critical of meta-narratives suggesting that "grand theories" tend to dismiss the naturally existing chaos which exists in the universe. He also suggested that meta-narratives were created and reinforced by power structures, which he felt, should not be trusted (Lyotard, 1979). Harvey suggested that meta-narratives were "grand stories" that *sought to explain reality in a way that allowed many individual ideas to fit together in a comprehensive whole* (Harvey, 1989). Both viewpoints have merit and therefore are not mutually exclusive. Great care should be exercised in the examination process of any suggested story beyond the obvious narrative. This work was meant to facilitate just such an examination.

The case for a meta-narrative of betrothal is based on Merriam Webster's Collegiate Dictionary which describes the word "meta" as *situated behind or beyond* (Webster, 1996). It is this notion that there exists a story of betrothal *behind or beyond* a simple narrative of a particular story in the Bible that is implied in the title of this chapter. It is that meta-narrative that ties the sixty-six books of the Bible together and allows the reader to view, for example, the books of Hosea and Ephesians, not as single pieces of literature, but as stories which fit within a grander story. The term meta-narrative is a compound word comprising the Greek word "meta" which means *among, with, or after* and "narrative" which means *a story that is told.*

Jewish history is filled with oral tradition. Long before the masses of the people could read and write, they were telling stories. An art form developed within the Jewish culture as can be seen in their folktales, fairy tales, fables, allegories, stories of miracles, etc. Schwartz described the passing of these stories from generation to generation as *a powerful cultural tradition which demonstrates that the events of our lives are meaningful* (Schwartz, 2000, recorded in Schram, 2000, p. xi). They have a beginning, middle, and an end. He cited collections of stories, such as The Arabian Nights, The Book of Jubilees, The Alphabet of Ben Sira, and The Book of Delight as being among the more than 20,000 stories spanning Jewish history assembled in the Israel Folktale Archives at the University of Haifa.

As one reads the stories of the Bible, the mind is left to imagine what the scene must have looked like. There are no photos or videos of the events recorded. This author hopes that a heavenly version of "instant replay" will be available in eternity.

Thankfully, the skills of great artists over the last several centuries have been able to render a visual impression of many of the Biblical stories. The masters' imagination brings the narrative to life and serves to reinforce our own limited concept of what the scene must have resembled. Many of these artworks are included in this manuscript to add a visual dimension to the research. Most are more than a century old and because of their age are found in the public domain and are found in the after material of this work.

Abraham's Probable Route to the Holy Land
Adam Clarke, c.1832
BibleNews1

CHAPTER TWO

THE NARRATIVE BEGAN IN UR

Ur of the Chaldees was indeed a beacon of light for culture and civilization in Abraham's day. Ur's influence on surrounding people groups of her era has been the focus of numerous studies in the last century. This research has been hindered primarily because of the uncertainty of Ur's location.

When Abraham appeared on the scene, in circa 1920 B.C., the Bible listed his dwelling place as Ur of the Chaldees (Genesis 11:31). The delineation in the Bible as being "of the Chaldees" clearly was meant to distinguish Abraham's Ur from another town, or towns with the same name. The city of אור – *Ur*, whose root name means "to be luminous or shine, or set on fire" (Strong's word, 1890), was located in either southern Mesopotamia or northern Mesopotamia.

There is considerable traditional support for the southern location of Ur, inland from what is now called the Persian Gulf. This location gained wide acceptance following a discovery of an inscribed brick in 1855 at Tel el-Muqqayyar by the English scholar Taylor. This site was excavated by the renowned archeologist C.L. Woolley from 1922-1934. Some Christian scholarship, however, has argued for alternative sites. Keil and Delitzsch suggested two possible locations: Ur of Ammian, located between Hatra and Nisibis, near Arrapachitis; or in Orhoi, Armenian Urrhai, the old name for Edessa, which is now called Urfa (Keil and Delitzsch, 1986). Kaiser, suggested a northern location, arguing that the term "Chaldees" could have only applied to the southern location eight hundred years after Abraham, or 1,000 B.C., while the

Chaldeans had lived in northern Mesopotamia much earlier (Kaiser, 2005).

Genesis 11:31 described how Abraham's caravan left Ur to go to the land of Canaan and that the journey brought them to Haran, where they dwelt for some time. Pritchard traces a probable route of march, from the traditional southern city of Ur, paralleling the Euphrates River from just west of Babylon, northwest toward Mari, continuing on to the river Ballkh, where a sharp turn north would have led the caravan to Haran (Pritchard, 1987). If the ultimate goal was Canaan, the trek to Haran from the southern city of Ur was hundreds of miles out of the way. A northern city of Ur would have made Haran more of a natural layover site.

The northern location of Ur would also be suggested by the Biblical account of Abraham selecting a bride for his son Isaac. He sent a servant from Canaan back to his own relatives to procure a wife for Isaac (Genesis 24:4). The location for the procurement was in Paddan-Aram, in northern Mesopotamia, further suggesting that southern Mesopotamia was not considered the ancestral home. Regardless of the actual location of the city of Ur, the Chaldean culture had a profound influence on the Jewish Patriarch and helped to shape traditions, heritage, and customs that have been passed down through Jewish history.

Abraham was not a young boy or adolescent, but a mature man in his seventies when he departed from Ur. He was seventy-five when he finally departed from Haran (Genesis 12:4). The journey to Canaan from Haran likely took the group south through Aleppo, Ebla, Qatna, Damascus, Hazor, then along the central ridge line from Shechem, Salem (Jerusalem), Hebron (Mamre) and on to Beersheba. The entire journey would have been dotted with locations for adequate water and towns located less than twenty miles apart (Pritchard,1987). There is no reference for the length of time that it took to make the journey. It would have certainly taken weeks traveling by camel and on foot with provisions. The scriptures speak of Abram and Sarai (Sar-a-i) being accompanied by Lot, his nephew and the "souls" that they had gotten in Haran (Genesis 12:5).

Abraham's Journey from Ur to Canaan
by Jozsef Molnar, c.1850
Hungarian National Gallery
Wikimedia Commons

Perception of the first Patriarch of the Bible has been shaped more by reference to the primitive conditions assumed in the early Bronze Age, and an assumed nomadic lifestyle akin to a Bedouin tribal culture; riding camels and sleeping under the open sky, scrounging for dates, figs, and minimal grain, while tending a small herd of goats on foreboding terrain. Woolley painted a drastically different perception of Abraham as having been reared in a long-established civilization that shared a "complex life of a great trade center" (Woolley, 1954, p.30). Although primitive by later standards, Ur was in its day a thriving center of commerce. Excavations in Ur have uncovered numerous houses with twelve to fourteen rooms. A street of private houses was excavated in the city of Ur in the 1920's. The houses were dated to 2100 B.C., which was about the time when Abraham was living there.

Excavated street in Ur dated to 2100 B.C.
Author's Archive

Woolley's findings showed that the common person dwelling at Ur led a material existence that was highly developed. Regardless of what a person's father's business might have been, Woolley suggested that work would have been conducted in *harmony with an elaborate system of commercial laws and precedents* (Woolley, 1954, p.42). Abraham would have grown up in this environment and would have been shaped by these laws and precedents. Woolley asserted that there was ample evidence in the Genesis

account of Abraham linking his actions to traditions long
held by the Sumerian people and recorded in such notable
texts as the Code of Hammurabi. This code, dated to circa
1900 B.C., was discovered in 1902 by Scheil at Susa (former
capital of the Elamites). It is now located in the Louvre in
Paris (Winton, 1958). There were other law codes that
were contemporaries of Hammurabi's, but only small parts
of these have been preserved. They would include the law
codes of King Lipit-Ishtar of Isin (c. 1868.B.C.), King Bilama
of Eshnunna (c. 1915 B.C.), and King Ur-Nammu of the Third
Dynasty of Ur (c. 2050 B.C.) (Hartman, 1963).

It is believed that Hammurabi based his code upon the
writings of a former King of Ur, named Dungi, who ruled in
the Third Dynasty period. During his reign, practically every
civil act was considered an act of law (Cook, 1903). These
acts were codified and sealed by witnesses. The documents
would have been carved on clay tablets and baked.

Code of Hammurabi Stone Tablet, c. 1754 BCE
The Louvre
Marie-Lan Nguyen, Photographer, 2006

Records were stored in a *genizah* or storeroom much like those found in Egypt. They have preserved a treasure trough of materials for archeologists to examine. These recorded civil acts included marriages, divorces, adoptions and legacies (Woolley, 1928).

The Burial of Sarah
Wood-engraving by Gustave Dore, 1866
Wikipedia Encyclopedia

Citing Abraham's purchase of the cave of Machpelah (Genesis 23:9) and his dealings with Hagar, Woolley suggested that Abraham often acted in accord with Sumerian law and offered as an example of this the reference to the cave purchase, where Abraham actually used the recognized currency of Babylon (Woolley, 1954, P.30). The culture, in which Abraham spent his first seven decades, reared her children in schools where reading, writing, arithmetic, and geometry were taught. Advanced training was available in medicine, astrology, and law. The evidence uncovered in Ur by Woolley's team determined that *from the beginning, Hebrew customs and beliefs were coloured and informed by the very old and a very artificial non-Semitic civilization* (Woolley, 1954, p. 43).

Abram and Sarai's journey to Canaan took place in what would be considered the golden years of a couple in the twenty-first century. Because of the longevity of those living in the age of the Patriarchs, seven decades of life would have placed them in the mid-life bracket. Still, they would have left Ur and ultimately Haran steeped in tradition, clinging to a value system they were shaped by, and ready to impart heritage and culture to their offspring.

In his later work entitled, "Abraham: Recent Discoveries", C.L. Woolley, when writing about Abraham's treatment of Hagar and Ishmael, suggested that Abraham was *bound by his upbringing.* Ur's ancient civilization was "engraved" in Abraham and Sarah, with its laws and traditions unable to be eradicated in them by a few years of living among a less sophisticated people. The archeologist concluded that, *there can be no doubt but that in the nomad tents, the life of the patriarch was guided and controlled by principles which Abraham had brought with him from his home in the civilized east* (Woolley, 1936, p.156). The assertion that tradition, forged in a civilized Ur, continued to shape Abraham's habits and actions throughout the remainder of his life, is supported by numerous Biblical narratives.

David Sees Bathsheba Bathing
by James Tissot, c.1896-1902
The Jewish Museum

CHAPTER THREE

SEXUAL RELATIONS IN ANCIENT TIMES

The second chapter of the Bible relays the story of the creation of the first women from the side of the man. Adam gave the name "woman" to the female gender and in verse 24 the scripture stated, *therefore shall a man leave his father and his mother and shall cleave unto his wife: and they shall be one flesh* (Genesis 2:24). The word "cleave" is translated from the Hebrew word דבק– *dabaq* – meaning "to catch by pursuit, be joined together, take or pursue" (Strong's word, 1692). From that point forward man has engaged in the practice of female conquest and marriage. Paleontologists have found evidence of these cultural practices around the world, even among the most primitive of peoples.

Every culture has developed cultural norms regarding the courtship process and ultimate joining of pairs. Betrothal rituals, wedding customs, processes of divorce and remarriage are all attested to (Hamon & Ingoldsby, 2004). The practice of taking multiple wives developed early and is first recorded in Genesis chapter four where Lamech is recorded as having two wives (Genesis 4:19).

It was not long before wicked practices began to manifest. Chapter six of Genesis records that the practice of taking wives of *all they chose* was the catalyst that led God to destroy the earth with a flood (Genesis 6:2-7). Only Noah and his three sons, with their wives, were spared the destruction and they survived to repopulate the earth. Generations passed before the recording of time would begin with any reliability. This record was initiated with the call of Abram circa 1920 B.C.

We have no record of the betrothal of Abram and his wife Sarai. The scripture simply states that Abram and his brother Nahor "took them wives." The Hebrew word translated "took" is the word לקח – *laqach* – meaning – "buy, carry away, accept, fetch, etc." (Strong's word, 3947). There is no Biblical account of the age of the couples, how they met, or whether they were related. The concept that Sarai was Abram's actual sister was reinforced by Abram's suggestion that he and Sarai tell the Pharaoh of Egypt that she was his sister (Genesis 12:13). He had feared that the Egyptian leader would kill him and take Sarai as his own. The lie was hatched and later repeated by Abraham's son, Isaac, in a similar scenario.

Abram's Counsel to Sarai
James Tissot, c 1896-1902
The Jewish Museum

Near relative marriages were common in the Antediluvian Period but not common in the Patriarchal Period. It is more likely that Sarai was Abram's half-sister or cousin. First cousin marriages are still practiced among some Hasidic communities and are legal in twenty states within the United States. Kershaw, writing in the New York Times, suggested that marriages to cousins account for up to ten percent of all marriages world-wide (Kershaw, 2009).

The Egyptian practice of bestowing gifts upon the family of a woman being courted is indicated by the same story about Abram. The Pharaoh saw that Sarai was beautiful and commanded that she be brought into his house. As a bride

Sarai is Taken to Pharaoh's Palace
James Tissot, c 1896-1902
The Jewish Museum

price, he gave Abram sheep, oxen, asses, camels and both menservants and maidservants thinking she was Abram's sister. The folly unraveled when God sent a plague upon Pharaoh's house. Sarai's chastity was kept intact only by the Lord's intervention (Genesis 12:14-20). Isaac must have heard this story as a child because he attempted the same trick with his wife Rebecca while living among the Philistines in Gerar (Genesis 26:7).

Long after Sarai's childbearing years had passed, she hatched a plan that would produce for her husband the offspring for which he longed. Abram fell to the temptation proposed by Sarai to go in to her maid Hagar so that she would conceive, and he would have an heir. God had promised him a son to continue his bloodline, but he had seen his wife's fertile years pass without conceiving. His lapse in trusting God to fulfill the promise was sufficient for his acquiescence to Sarai and her plan to gain merit. Hagar had not come into Abram's house with a dowry or contract. She was elevated above the status of handmaid as she became the mother of his firstborn. It was not an uncommon practice in his day.

Sarah Leading Hagar to Abraham
by Matthias Stom, c.1639
Wikimedia Commons

The term "concubine" in Hebrew is the word פילגש –
piylegesh – referring to a marital companion of inferior status
to that of a wife (Strong's word, 6370; Encyclopedia Judaica
Vol. 5, p 862). The term is etymologically derived from the
Aramaic transliterated words *palga isha*, which means half-
wife. Hartman described a concubine as a wife of second
rank who continued to live in her own father's house, but
who would be visited on a regular basis for conjugal relations
(Hartman, 1963).

Hagar was not technically a concubine. The term "maid"
used in the scripture is the Hebrew word שפחה – *shiphchah*
– meaning "female slave, or woman servant" (Strong's word,
8198). She bore Abram a son named Ishmael, which meant

Abraham Dismissing Hagar and Ishmael
by Barent Fabritius, c.1660
The Metropolitan Museum of Art

"God will hear." The name was Abram's attempt to justify his act as fulfillment of God's promise to him. The mother of Abram's child was rejected by Sarai for disrespect and Sarai insisted that Abram send both the slave and the child away. Again, drawing upon cultural norms from his upbringing, the handmaiden and her child were forced out of Abram's household. This was no simple issue for Abram for he loved the child and for a dozen years raised him as his only child.

Hagar would later return to Abraham's house after Sarah's death and would have her name and status changed. Abraham's act of taking Hagar back into his household would be consistent with the scriptural injunction that if a man has slept with a woman, he should marry her (Deuteronomy 22:28-29). Her name would become הרוטק– Keturah – which comes from a root word meaning "to perfume or fumigate in a close place so as to drive out the occupants" (Strong's word, 6999). She and her son had been occupants of his tent and, to appease Sarai, had been driven out. She would become Abraham's second wife (Meyer, 1906, p312-322; Montgomery, 1934, p42-45, Ginzberg, 1964, p375).

Keturah would bare him six additional sons. Their names and meaning were: זמורן – *Zimran* (celebrate: from the root word "to strike with the fingers" as if playing an instrument), יקשן – *Jokshan* (fowler: from the root word "to ensnare"), מדן – *Medan* (discord or strife), מדין – *Midian* (brawling or contention), ישבק – *Ishbak* (he will leave), and שוה – *Shuah* (depression from the root word "to sink") (Genesis 25:2). These children would not share the inheritance that Isaac was afforded by his bloodline. Instead, these offspring of Keturah/Hagar would be given gifts and sent across the Jordan River eastward. There, they would become the fathers of the Arab nations.

Of particular interest is the use of the plural word "concubines" when referring to the children being sent eastward. The scripture states, *But unto the sons of the concubines, which Abraham had, Abraham gave gifts, and sent them away from Isaac his son, while he yet lived...* (Genesis 25:6). The meaning may suggest that there were other concubines for Abraham, but this was not clear from the Biblical narrative. His age and continued virility would be factors that would affect this.

Royal concubines would become common features in Jewish history during the period of the Kings of Israel and Judah. King Solomon was the most notorious participant in this practice as the scriptures record that he had *threescore queens, and fourscore concubines, and virgins without number* (Song of Solomon 6:8).

Solomon and His Harem
by James Tissot, c.1870
The Jewish Museum

There was no rite associated with taking a concubine or mating with a female slave. There was a provision in ancient Assyria where a concubine could gain the rank of wife, but only after a special ceremony in which the man publicly veiled her in the presence of witnesses (Roth, 1995; Assyrian code A, 41, recorded in the Encyclopedia Judaica, vol. 5, p. 860). This act of veiling a woman was an established tradition among many people groups and has endured in numerous cultures.

All three monotheistic religions have adopted veils in some form or fashion. Orthodox Jewish women have the tradition of covering their hair with what in Yiddish is called a טיכעל – *tichel* – head scarf and veil their face during the wedding day ritual known as *badeken.* Eastern Orthodox Christians and many Roman Catholic women cover their hair with chapel veils when attending a liturgical service. Christian brides typically have veils over their faces for the beginning of their wedding ceremonies. Catholic nuns don their habits in public, while Moslem women use head scarfs in less observant societies and full coverings called برقع – *burqa* in the more observant Islamic cultures.

Mating with the slaves of your wife continued after Abraham and is recorded in the story of Jacob. He mated with the handmaidens of both Rachel and Leah (Bilhah and Zilpah) and they each bore him two sons (Genesis 30:4-13). The sons' status was not diminished and all four are included as the head of four of the twelve tribes of Israel: namely, Dan, Naphtali, Gad, and Asher.

Jacob's prophetic words to each of them have latent marriage covenant meaning. To Dan he ends his words with, *I have waited for thy salvation, O Lord* (Genesis 49:18), which according to the Jerusalem Targum, was a Messianic

Rachel and Leah
by James Tissot, c.1870
The Jewish Museum

expression meaning *for thy redemption my soul waits* (Extract of Fagius in the London Polyglot, quoted by Keil & Delitzsch, Vol. 1, p. 404). The concept of a groom redeeming his bride is entrenched in Judaism, and the notion of the tribe longing for her redeemer is implied.

Gad was told that he would *overcome at the last* (Genesis 49:19). An unusual triple alliteration is used in the verse (גד גדוד יגודנו – *gad gadud ygudnu*). The root word for overcome is גוד – *guwd*. It literally means "to crowd upon or press into." Although used as a military expression to "overcome a troop," it has metaphorical connotations of consummation.

Asher was told that he would *yield royal dainties* (Genesis 49:20) and he inherited some of the most fertile soil in the promised land lying along the Mediterranean Sea from the Carmel range north to Tyre. Pleasure is the root meaning for the Hebrew expression – מעדני-מלך – *maadanei melech*.

"To live voluptuously or to delight self" is the way Strong translated the root (Strong's words, 5727 and 4574). This type of living is characterized by unrestrained pleasure to the senses and sensuous enjoyment (Webster, 1996).

Naphtali was told that he was a *hind let loose: he giveth goodly words* (Genesis 49:21). The Hebrew word for hind is אילה – *ayalah* – which is "a female deer or doe" (Strong's word, 355). A derivative is used in Proverbs 5:19 where it states, *Let her be as the loving hind and pleasant doe; let her breasts satisfy thee at all times; and be thou ravished always with her love.*

Taking wives by force was also something that is recorded from the Biblical period. The book of Judges records the story of the battle between the tribe of Benjamin and the children of Israel. More than 43,000 Benjamites were killed at the hand of their brothers. The men of Israel swore an oath in Mizpeh that they would not give their daughters to be married to the remaining men of the tribe of Benjamin. They later lamented this decision saying, *How shall we do for wives for them that remain, seeing we have sworn by the Lord that we will not give them our daughters to wives* (Judges 21:7)?

The solution to this dilemma came in two forms. First, the men and married women of Ja'–besh-gil'-e-ad were killed for not standing with Israel. Four hundred young virgins from the town were saved alive and given to the men of Benjamin to take for wives (Judges 21:12). The second solution was to have the men of Benjamin who did not have a wife, lay in wait outside the city of Shiloh. There was an annual feast among the inhabitants of that region in which the young maidens would come out to dance in the vineyards. The Benjamites were told to *catch you every man his wife of the daughters of Shiloh and go to the land of Benjamin* (Judges 21:21). The men of Israel promised to defend this action against the complaints of the maiden's fathers, and thus the tribe of Benjamin continued to produce heirs.

This story is eerily similar to the ancient story known as the rape of the Sabine women. It supposedly occurred early in Roman history when Roman men sought unsuccessfully to negotiate with the Sabine leadership for the right to marry the daughters of the Sabines. A festival was arranged and on cue, the Roman men stole the Sabine women. The Latin word *rapere* means abduction. It is translated as the word "rape", which now implies sexual violation rather than mere abduction (Webster, 1996).

Forbidden relationships were also a part of the ancient culture. The story of Judah and Tamar is a classic example. The story is found in Genesis and depicts Tamar, who was the daughter-in-law to Judah, who veiled herself and posed

The Rape of the Sabine Women
by Pietro da Cortona, c.1627
Wikimedia Commons

as a harlot. Judah, lured by her, but not knowing it was
his daughter-in-law, slept with her and she conceived
twins (Genesis 38:13-26). The worlds' oldest profession is
mentioned in this text as if it were culturally acceptable or
at the least an understandable practice. The story of Judah
and Tamar dates to circa 1729 B.C., but prostitution was
well established centuries earlier as attested by the Code
of Hammurabi which included provisions to protect the
inheritance rights of prostitutes (Hartman, 1963).

Judah and Tamar
by Horace Vernet, c.1840
Wikimedia Commons

Later Mosaic laws would specifically forbid such a
relationship. The eighteenth chapter of Leviticus is devoted
to outlining those relationships that are expressly forbidden
and the Bible often described the violations of these laws.
Examples of such violations would include, but not be
limited to, the following examples: דינה – *Dinah (justice)*, the
daughter of Leah was defiled by שכם – *Shechem* the Hivite

(root means "to incline the shoulder to a burden or heavy load"). He was an uncircumcised pagan and this act was described as having *wrought folly in Israel* (Genesis 34:7). The term "folly" was used of shameful sins of the flesh. Keil and Delitzsch describe the seduction of Dinah as a "crime against Israel for having ignored the unique relationship between Israel and God" (Keil & Delitzsch, Vol.1 p.312).

Shechem and his father Hamor spoke to Dinah's father (Jacob) and told him that Shechem would pay whatever dowry was asked. Dinah's brothers tricked them by demanding circumcision as a pretext to giving Jewish daughters as their brides. Simeon and Levi avenged their sister on the third day after the procedure and killed all the men of the town because of the defilement. This act of retribution was not appreciated by Jacob.

Seduction of Dinah, Daughter of Leah
by James Tissot, c.1896-1902
The Jewish Museum

Potiphar's wife made an advance on Joseph, but it was refused. Joseph asked her, *How can I do this great*

wickedness, and sin against God (Genesis 39:9)? The
Hebrew word for wickedness is the word רע – *ra* – which
means *evil* and comes from the root meaning "to spoil by
breaking into pieces" (Strong's word, 7489). Joseph was

Joseph and Potiphar's Wife
by Guido Reni, c.1626
Wikimedia Commons

more interested in preserving his relationship with God than
engaging with the carnal pleasure manifested before him.
Joseph fled the scene and was later to be imprisoned by
the false charge made by the scorned woman. His example
would be immortalized in the New Testament imperative to
flee fornication (I Corinthians 6:18). The Greek word φεύγω
– *pheugo* – is translated "flee" in the verse. It is a prime verb
meaning "to run away, shun, escape, or vanish" (Strong's
word, 5343). Paul was commanding that one should run from
πορνεία – *porneia* – a term that literally means "harlotry, but
includes adultery, incest and fornication in general" (Strong's
word, 4202). Note that the English word pornography stems
from this Greek term.

Such was not the case with Jacob's first-born son named Reuben. He was the son of Leah but disgraced himself when he slept with his father's concubine Bilhah. Judgment for his action was not a death sentence, but rather a curse pronounced when Jacob gave his prophecy over his twelve sons. It is recorded in Genesis 49:4 and states, ...*unstable as water, thou shalt not excel; because thou wentest up to thy father's bed; then defiledst thou it: he went up to my couch.* The land of his inheritance would be restricted to a small section around what today is called Jaffa, and his tribe would be excluded from the list of tribes in the Book of Revelation where 144,000 are sealed (Revelation 7:5-8).

In the period of the Kings, Saul reneged on his promise to give David his oldest daughter Merab. A betrothal is implied in the scriptures as David was asked to simply fight the Lord's battles as payment for the right to be the King's son-in-law. When the time was at hand for the wedding, Saul chose to give Merab to another man. The scripture does not allude to the breach of this covenant but proceeds to tell the story of how Saul conspired to ensnare David by giving him another daughter named Michal. David would provide the bride price of a hundred foreskins of the Philistines for this privilege (I Samuel 18:20-27).

King David historically has been viewed as a worshiper, a valiant warrior, and great leader of the Israelites. His moral lapse with Bathsheba, which led to adultery and murder, tarnished his stature and brought shame upon him, but did not result in judgment warranted by the Mosaic Law. Both offenses were punishable by death, but David was a sitting king and had the respect and love of the Jewish people. His indiscretion and premeditated act of murder has largely been relegated to a minor footnote in David's life story.

David's children followed in their father's wicked ways. His first-born son Amnon raped his half-sister Tamar. She fled, defiled and shamed, and her brother Absalom took vengeance and had Amnon slain. David was informed of the death by his nephew Joadab who stated, *for by the appointment of Absalom this hath been determined from the day that he forced his sister Tamar* (II Samuel 13:32).

Amnon and Tamar
by Jan Steen, c.1650
Wikimedia Commons

CHAPTER FOUR

BETROTHAL IN ANCIENT TIMES

The rite of betrothal in ancient times can be glimpsed in Assyrian, Sumerian, and Phoenician cultures (Pomeroy, 1975). The fact that Abraham was closely influenced by Sumerian culture can be seen in his fulfilling the obligation of the father in the mate selection process for Isaac. Abraham was *old and well stricken in age* when the time came to select a bride for his son (Genesis 24:1). Abraham was one hundred years old when Isaac was born and Isaac was forty years old when he married Rebecca, thus Abraham was 140 when it was time to select the mate. The responsibility was his and it is understood that had he been a younger man, he himself would have gone to fetch a bride for his son. As it occurred, Abraham had his oldest servant (Eliezer) swear an oath that he would not take a bride for Isaac from among the pagans around him, but would travel back to Abraham's kindred to find the bride for the heir (Genesis 24:1-67).

This act was part of the heritage Abraham had enjoyed. It was one of many customs or traditions that predated Mosaic Law. It would be several centuries before the Torah would give legal sanction to the customs that were already in practice. Bader, quoting the Rashbam-Samuel Ben Meir, states that *The Torah merely strengthened the accepted conduct and insured the future observance of these laws* (Bader, 1988, p. 423). Traditions tend to morph over time and the tradition of the father selecting the mate for a child certainly was no exception. By the Period of the Judges, a slight shift was detected in the bride selection process. Eight centuries after Abraham, the scriptures relate the story of Samson's quest for a wife. His father Manoah had only a ceremonious role in the selection.

The Wedding of Samson
by Rembrandt van Rijn, c.1638
Wikimedia Commons

Chapter fourteen of the book of Judges begins by stating that Samson had seen a Philistine woman in the town of תמנה – *Timnath*. The Hebrew name for the town means: "a portion assigned." Its root comes from the word "manna" (Strong's word, 8553).   In the end of the story, it becomes clear that the selection of this woman was in the plan of the Lord. This would make the woman the portion assigned and would have spiritual implications with regard to destiny. The later Jewish concept of destiny would be cemented in the Yiddish expression באשערת – *beshert* – often translated as "soul mate," but more accurately defined as "inevitable, predestined, or meant to be" (Weinreich, 1968, p. 703).

Samson had troubled his parents with the news that he had found a gentile woman that pleased him. He told his father, *now therefore get her for me to wife* (Judges 14:2). He repeated the command to his father in the following verse reiterating; *get her for me; for she pleaseth me well* (Judges 14:3). Together with his parents, Samson made the journey to Timnath and Samson talked to the woman. It was only *after a time* (Judges 14:8) that they returned to take her. The tradition is alluded to in verse ten of the chapter as it reads, *So his father went down unto the woman: and Samson made there a feast; for so used the young men to do* (Judges 14:10). This action is consistent with the later established traditions of a visitation to arrange a marriage and a period of time between the betrothal and the actual wedding ceremony.

The Wedding at Cana
by Paolo Veronese, c.1563
Wikimedia Commons

When the time came for a father to contract for a wife for his son, the father would schedule a time to meet with the father of the bride-to-be. It was the father's responsibility to select the mate and arrange for the actual betrothal of their children (Khodadad, 1926; Epstein, 1927). The meeting would take place at the home of the father of the bride-to-be because formal betrothal took place in the house of the bride's father (Scott, 1995).

The Unequal Marriage
by Vasily Pukirev, c.1862
Wikimedia Commons

There is no direct indication of the age of Samson when he initiated the action to procure a wife, nor is there indication of the age of the Philistine woman he wanted. It was understood by early sages that a man needed to give his sons and daughters in marriage immediately as they approached maturity, so as to prevent their temptation to

engage in the commission of adultery or pre-marital sex
(Ganzfried, 1928). The age varied from culture to culture.

In ancient Greece (circa 500 B.C.), it was the common
practice for girls to marry by the age of fifteen, and often to
men twice their age (Cantarella, 1987). The same practice
was common in Jewish history. Blomberg suggests that men
were regularly married by the age of eighteen and normally to
women who had just hit puberty (Blomberg, 1997). Although
love was a possible reason for marriage, the culture of the
time viewed love as something that would follow in marriage
(Hartman, 1963).

There were early Talmudic sages who tried to influence
change in the extremes of this practice. Rav Abba Arecha
of Sura in Babylon wrote in the Mid Second Century that a
man shouldn't marry off his daughter when she is too young
to know whom she would like to marry (Babylonian Talmud,
Kiddushin 41a, quoted in Bader, 1988). He would later forbid
the marriage of one's daughter to an old man (Babylonian
Talmud, Sanhedrin 77b, quoted in Bader, 1988). This was
a far cry from the time of Isaac, who was forty when he took
Rebecca as his bride, or the story of King David, who was
dying when his servants brought in a young virgin named
אבישג – Abishag for him to *lie in thy bosom* (1 Kings 1:2).

Abishag's name comes from a compound root word
combining the words "father" and "to stray, to sin through
ignorance, or to be ravished" – thus culminating with the
expression, "father of error" (Strong's word, 49). David was
too old to copulate with the young virgin, but she remained
in the royal household after David's death and was later the
center of the controversy that led to the death of Adonijah (I
Kings 2:21-25).

The ancient ceremony of marriage in the Jewish culture occurred in two distinct ceremonies. The first was the betrothal ritual called either קדושין – *kiddushin* – which comes from the root meaning "holy" or ארושן – *erusin* – "betrothal." In the early Talmudic period, and perhaps centuries prior to this period, betrothal occurred with the bridegroom, in the presence of two witnesses, handing over to his bride-to-be any object of value while reciting the marriage formula:

הני את מקדשת לי בטבעת זו | כדת משה וישראל

Behold you are consecrated unto me with this ring according to the law of Moses and Israel. This would also involve the blessing over and consumption of a glass of wine (Encyclopedia Judaica, Vol. 11 p.1033).

A goblet of wine being passed to the bride is mentioned in the Encyclopedia Judaica as part of this ritual (Encyclopedia Judaica, Vol. 11, p. 1034). In the Apocryphal book of I Maccabees, which is dated to the Second Century before Christ, there is description of an elaborate procession for a bridal couple accompanied by music and great celebration (I Maccabees 9:39).

A written agreement, called a תנאים – *tenaim* – the Hebrew word for conditions, containing all settlements and conditions agreed upon by the parents of the groom and bride would be drawn up and signed by the future groom and bride (Goldin, 1956, Isaacson, 1979). Many such agreements have survived from antiquity. In ancient times these included the provision of food, clothing, and other necessities as well as a commitment to engage in conjugal relations. It also pledged to the wife a fixed amount as a settlement in the event of the dissolution of the marriage (Epstein, 1927).

Legal Document
Dated to 139 A.D. on vellum
Author's Archive

The second part of the ancient marriage ceremony would not take place for a set period of time (usually a year for a virgin). The second ceremony was called either נישוין – *Nissu'in* (marriage proper) or חופה – *Chuppah* (a reference to the canopy that actual vows were exchanged under). Until the destruction of the Temple in 70 A.D., both the bride and the groom wore distinctive headdresses and the bride would be veiled (Encyclopedia Judaica, Vol. 11, p.1033).

Scott has shown that the ancient betrothal ritual took place in the home of the father of the bride-to-be (Scott, 1995). Edersheim, writing concerning ancient pilgrim festivals, suggested that these were the perfect times for parents to arrange their children's weddings (Edersheim, 1883). Regardless of whether the occasion was in the clan home of the bride-to-be, or at a temporary dwelling place celebrating a festival, the father of the groom-to-be and his son would make a visit to arrange for the hand of the

bride, and this would be done with the bride-to-be's father or
nearest male kin (like in the case of Rebecca's brother).

Jewish headdress
Jewish Virtual Library

Ideally, the father and his son would arrive and be
ushered into the dwelling. The custom of washing the feet
of the visitor may very well have been enacted in ancient
times, but the focus was on the importance of the business
that needed to be addressed (Edersheim, 1883). There
would be a total of four cups of wine partaken of in the
ritual of betrothal and marriage. In the Middle Ages the two
ceremonies were combined into one, but in the Biblical period
the two ceremonies were distinct.

On the occasion of the betrothal, the first cup was filled
with wine and drank as a toast to set apart the occasion as
something significant. Each of the feasts of Israel, every
Sabbath, and special life events in Judaism all begin with a
cup of wine and a blessing sanctifying the event. This act is
known as קידוש – *Kiddush*, which literally means sanctification

(from Strong's word, 6942). In the betrothal act, men had come to ask for the hand of a daughter of the house. It was

Wedding Procession, Jodhpur
by Edwin Lord Weeks, c.1892
Wikimedia Commons

not a common event for the household, it was special, set apart as unique, and considered a holy act with significant repercussions. To begin this special moment with a *Kiddush*, would elevate the event as something that is holy before the Lord. The Kiddush custom calls for the head of the house to intone the blessing for wine, then sip from the cup, and pass it to those in attendance (Isaacson, 1979). It is called the cup of sanctification.

Khodadad argued that in ancient times parents would have been guided by two considerations when considering a bridegroom for their daughter. They would first want to keep her within their clan or "circle of her kindred," such as when

Laban told Jacob, *it is better that I give her to thee, than that I should give her to another man* (Genesis 29:19). Should they have to give her to someone outside the clan, the parents would need to consider potential tribal complications arising from the union; in particular, the impact of transferring, in the absence of a male heir, the real property from one clan to another. Secondly, the parents would give consideration for what the loss of a daughter would mean to their immediate way of life. The daughter would normally tend the flocks of her father. With her absent from the home, the family would need to accommodate the loss (Khodadad, 1926).

In the ancient betrothal ritual, after the cup of sanctification was partaken, the second cup, the cup of salvation, would be filled with wine, but not immediately imbibed. It was now time for the father of the bride-to-be to elaborate about his daughter. He would speak about the character of his daughter, her talents, and skills. He would speak in detail about what her chores were around the house and how her absence would bring him great distress. The father of the bride-to-be was establishing a level of worth from which he would negotiate a price for his daughter (Khodadad, 1926). He would not wish to settle for a nominal price. He was about to lose a valuable asset in his household. The fathers would then negotiate an agreed price that would be paid for the girl. To seal the agreement, both men would partake of the second cup of wine. The betrothal agreement has been highlighted in books, plays, and movies since the turn of the 20th Century when Sholem Aleichem wrote *Tevye the Dairyman* about Jewish life in Russia; a notable example is *Fiddler on the Roof.*

Once the price was thoroughly negotiated, the terms would be codified in the תנאים – *tenaim.* The famous sage, known as the Gaon of Vilna, wrote that, *it is preferable to dissolve the bond of marriage by divorce than to break an engagement* (Sefer Sha'are Rahanim, quoted in Goldin, 1956, p. 2).

In ancient Sumer, the actual betrothal was signaled by the presentation of gifts from the groom-to-be to the father of the bride-to-be. In the Biblical account of Eliezer negotiating for the hand of Rebecca, he had planned in advance, and brought with his caravan gifts for both Rebecca's mother and her brother (Genesis 24:53). This was a traditional gesture reflecting Abraham's dependence upon Sumerian culture. This gift would be forfeited if the father of the bride-to-be broke off the engagement, but the groom-to-be could recover double price in the event his betrothed broke off the engagement. Woolley suggested that this custom developed from a much earlier practice known as "marriage by purchase" (Woolley, 1928, p.100).

Compensation for the parents for the loss of the help of their daughter was paid by the groom-to-be. This compensation was called מהר – *mohar* – or the "purchase price." It is one of two terms translated "dowry" in the Old Testament. Its root meaning implies "a readiness to bargain for a wife" (Strong's word, 4119). It is used three times in the scriptures.

In Genesis 34:12, Shechem, son of Hamor the Hivite, petitioned Jacob for the hand of his daughter Dinah (who had been raped by Shechem). Shechem told Jacob that whatever price would be asked, he would give it. Exodus 22:17 describes a *dowry of virgins,* which is the price for a virgin that had been defiled but whose betrothal was denied the perpetrator. The third occasion for its use occurred in I Samuel 18:25, when David is told that in lieu of a dowry Saul would accept a hundred foreskins of the Philistines for his daughter's hand. Contrast this with the other term used to translate the word dowry in the Old Testament. That word is זבד – *zebed* – meaning "to confer a gift" (Strong's word, 2065). It is only used once in the scriptures in Genesis 30:20, when Leah had delivered her sixth son for Jacob. Her response was that God had *endued* her with a good dowry, suspecting that Jacob would now be obligated to dwell with her.

Although it was possible to be paid in actual money, the *mohar* could also be paid in personal service. The story of Jacob working seven years for the price for Rachel is a good example of this (Genesis 29:18-30). Laban tricked Jacob and after Jacob had served him seven years, Laban gave him Leah instead of Rachel on his wedding night. After fulfilling Leah's week as a new bride, he married Rachel also, having promised Laban to work an additional seven years for her. This meant paying the *mohar* after the marriage had been consummated.

Once the man paid the agreed price, the woman became his property. He was viewed as her בעל – *baal* – meaning "master or husband." Its root concept is "to have dominion over" (Strong's word, 1167). She would henceforth be viewed as one possessed by an owner (Hartman, 1963). Harris suggested that a thorough understanding of the term *baal* could not be complete without seeing it from a theological standpoint. Namely, as marriage terminology employed by God to define his relationship to his people (Harris, 1980). Examples from the scriptures would be Isaiah 54:5 where the scriptures record, *for your maker is your husband.* Additionally, the Prophet Jeremiah records the Lord stating, *For I am a husband unto you* (Jeremiah 3:14).

The tradition of paying the *mohar* changed during the later period of the Hasmoneans when the head of the Pharisees, Simeon ben Shatach, enacted measures that allowed poorer Israelites to simply record in the marriage contract the *mohar* price, rather than having to actually pay it. This reform made marriage easier and divorce harder as it made the woman an equal partner in all of the groom's possessions (Shabbat 12b, quoted in Bader, 1988).

In the ancient betrothal ceremony, the groom-to-be became the redeemer of the bride-to-be. He would do so by paying the agreed bride price. In ancient Babylon, the bride price was an act of good faith, which sealed the groom's right to the bride. More literally, it sealed the family of the groom's right to the bride. If the groom died following the betrothal but before the wedding, his father could insist that the bride be given to one of the groom's brothers. The bride married into her husband's family and not simply an individual. The bride price could be paid in installments, and there is evidence that portions could be delayed until the birth of the first child (Stone, 1992).

Once the bride price was agreed upon, the terms of the agreement would be codified. The bride-to-be would be brought forth to hear the reading of the כתבה – *Ketubah* – which is the marriage contract that included the *Tenaim* (conditions). It would outline the financial obligations the husband would undertake toward his bride-to-be. In essence, it is a memorandum of the obligation which a husband assumes toward his wife at the time of marriage. Betrothal involved both financial and legal implications and could be the subject of extended negotiations. It would include the groom's responsibilities and the amount of money she would receive at his death or in case of divorce (Scott, 1995). The

Ketubah provided a settlement of at least 200 denars for a maiden, 100 denars for a widow, while the priestly council at Jerusalem fixed 400 denars for a priest's daughter (Edersheim, 1883). In Hammurabi's code a woman was not considered married unless a contract was drawn up between the bride and groom (Richardson, 2000).

In ancient Athens (circa 500 B.C.), a public pledge was made by the couple. It would be witnessed by family and friends. An unusual feature of the ceremony involved the bride's dowry being laid down for all to see. Once handed over, the couple was considered betrothed (West, 2000). The father of the bride was bound to provide a dowry for his daughter conformable to her station in life. The dowry, whether money, property, or jewelry was identified in the marriage contract and belonged to the wife, the husband being obliged to add to it one half more (Edersheim, 1883, Schlesinger, 1987). Stone found that the dowry consisted of household utensils, silver rings, slaves and property. In later periods, dowries would include furniture, textiles, and jewelry (Stone, 1992).

Pritchard records an ancient marriage contract belonging to a Jew of Elephantine from 459 B.C., entitled, *Mibtahiah's first marriage*, in which the father of the bride, Mahseiah ben Yedoniah, codifies the dowry he will pay to the future son-in-law, Jezaniah ben Uriah. Among the items given is a house laying west of the house belonging to Jeziariah. In the Ketubah it states: *build and equip that site... and dwell thereon with your wife, but you may not sell that house or give it as a present to others, only your children by my daughter Mibtahiah shall have power over it after you two* (Pritchard, 1969, p. 222).

A Bedouin Woman with her Dowry, c.1900
Author's Archive

Nejat and Rhea described an ancient document found at Ur, which recorded the expenses, gifts, and payments incurred by a prospective father of the bride. The document described the negotiations as having taken place over four months and was divided into four phases: 1) betrothal, 2) payments of both the bride's dowry and the groom's bride price, 3) the bride's move to her father-in-law's house, and 4) consummation of the marriage (Nejat and Rhea, 1998).

In the ancient betrothal rite, a third cup would be filled with wine. Once the Ketubah was read aloud, the groom-to-be would drink from this cup called the cup of redemption. The bride-to-be would then be asked the same question that Rebecca had been asked, namely, *wilt thou go with this man*? (Genesis 24:58). If she said yes, the forthcoming marriage could move forward. She would then drink from the same cup of wine. The agreement having been toasted, the vessel was then broken to signify that, *just as a broken vessel can never be repaired, so is a broken engagement irreparable* (Goldin, 1956).

At this point they were legally betrothed and considered married in every aspect but physical consummation (Edersheim, 1886). The ceremony finalized the marriage agreement and the marriage contract was handed over to the bride-to-be (Friedman, 1986). An ancient Aramaic Papyri dating to 459 B.C. in Elephantine records the words of a groom-to-be in his Ketubah to the father of his would-be wife: *I have come to your house that you might give me your daughter Mibtahiah in marriage. She is my wife and I am her husband from this day for ever. I have given you as the bride price of your daughter Mibtahiah a sum of five shekels, royal weight. It has been received by you and your heart is content therewith* (translated by Ginsberg, 1969, quoted in Pritchard, 1969, p.222).

Once the betrothal was in effect, the bride's world was forever changed. She would continue to live under her father's roof until the day of the marriage ceremony, but her identity was no longer wrapped up in her father's clan. It was now wrapped in the clan of the family into which she was marrying. Her needs were now the responsibility of the groom-to-be and his family (Stone, 1992). Her debts were now his debts. His wealth was now her wealth. Her future was no longer in her father's house, although she would remain there for a time while her beloved prepared the dwelling they would share. Harris provided a variant viewpoint suggesting that the husband was incorporated into the tribe of his wife, further stating that the children were considered as belonging to her tribe (Harris, 1980). This was not the procedure in the Biblical period.

The betrothal event would involve the giving of gifts to the bride. This is seen in the story of Isaac's bride-to-be. Rebecca was given a golden earring, bracelets, and ten shekels of gold, followed by jewels of silver, jewels of gold, and raiment (Genesis 24:22,53). For centuries, the practice of exchanging rings has been practiced. Although 21st century traditions are of later origin, the practice of giving jewelry stems from the account of Isaac and Rebecca.

Common Jewish wedding ring inscribed with
I am my beloved's: my beloved is mine – אני לדודי ודודי לי

Multiple liturgies have evolved around the actual exchange of rings. The Anglican Church lists within its Book of Common Prayer, dated to 1662, the following stanza to be read as the ring is given, *With this ring I thee wed, with my body I thee worship, and with all my worldly goods I thee endow. In the name of the Father, and of the Son, and of the Holy Ghost* (Church of England's Book of Common Prayer, 1662). It should be noted that it is the groom that places a ring on his bride's left-hand ring finger. The bride does not place a ring on the groom's finger in the Anglican tradition.

Eastern Orthodox Christians exchange rings at betrothal and not at the wedding ceremony. The groom's ring is made of gold and the bride's ring is made of silver. A priest is asked to bless the rings with holy water and the rings are worn on the left-hand ring finger. They are first held over the couple's heads as the priest proclaims, *The servant of God* (name is spoken) *is betrothed to the handmaid of God* (name is spoken), *in the name of the Father, and of the Son, and of the Holy Spirit. Amen* (Hapgood, 1975, p.604).

In the modern Orthodox Jewish wedding ceremony, the groom recites in Hebrew the expression, *with this ring, you are consecrated to me according to the law of Moses and Israel:* הרי את מקדשת לי בטבעת זו כדת משה וישראל

The ring is then placed on the forefinger of the bride's right hand because this finger is closest to the blood flow to the heart (Goldin, 1956).

There would likely be a pledge to prepare the dwelling, perhaps plan the actual date for the wedding. The event would conclude with instructions that if the bride should need anything, the responsibility was now her future husband's and his family to provide that need (West, 2000).

The giving of gifts was not simply reserved for the bride-to-be. Genesis 24:53 told the account of Eliezer, the eldest servant in the house of Abraham, whom the patriarch sent to obtain a wife for Abraham's son Isaac. In the narrative, the servant gave gifts to Rebekah as well as precious things to her brother Laban and to her mother. Such a gift is called a מטן – *mattan*.

From the moment the ceremony was performed, the couple was considered husband and wife in the eyes of the law and the community. The bond could only be dissolved by a bill of divorce or by death (Kholdadad, 1926). Breach of faithfulness was regarded as adultery; and the property of the woman became virtually that of her betrothed, unless he had expressly renounced it (Edersheim, 1883). It was the seriousness of this covenant and the prescribed punishment

Rebecca and Eliezer at the Well
by Carlo Maratta, c.1655
The Indianapolis Museum of Art

outlined in the Torah that led Joseph to have such misgivings about following through with his planned marriage to Mary the mother of Jesus. She was pregnant after the betrothal was made and Joseph knew it was not his child. The gospel of Matthew describes Joseph as being, *a just man, and not willing to make her a public example.* Although he had the right to have her exposed as an adulterer and stoned to death, he desired to *put her away privily* (Matthew 1:19).

Intervention came in the form of a dream in which an angel appeared to Joseph and explained that the child was *of the Holy Ghost* (Matthew 1:20).

As the New Testament begins, the story of Mary and Joseph would suggest that Joseph was much older than Mary. He had children from a previous marriage (Mark 6:3) and likely passed away when Jesus was a teenager. He is not mentioned after the early chapters of the Gospels, but Mary is seen throughout the life of Jesus. McNeile, when citing the episode where Jesus was rejected in Nazareth, suggests that in the Greek translation of Matthew 13:55, the expression οὐχ οὗτός ἐστιν ὁ τοῦ τέκτονος υἱόσ is better translated, *he whom we used to know as the carpenter's son,* and supports the notion that Joseph was already dead by that point in time (McNeile, 1980).

In the case of Mary and Joseph, Edersheim suggests that they were both so poor that their betrothal ceremony must have been simple and the dowry small. This was suggested based upon the type of offering brought to the Temple at the occasion of the dedication of Jesus. He distinguished betrothal in Galilee from that which was common in Judea. In the Galilee area they were "more simple" in nature (Edersheim, 1883).

The Betrothal of the Holy Virgin and Saint Joseph
by James Tissot, c.1886-1894
Brooklyn Museum

As the wedding day approached, the bride-to-be would visit the מקוה – *Mikvah* – "a pool of running water used for ritual purification" (Encyclopedia Judaica, Vol. 11, p. 1534). She would be attended by her mother and would immerse herself naked into the flowing water (Greenberg, 1989). A transition was being made by this act. A transition from the single life to the life of a married woman.

On the Sabbath before the ceremony, it became the custom of having the groom-to-be read from the Torah Scroll in the synagogue. The Talmud states that King Solomon had built a special gate in the Temple for bridegrooms, where the inhabitants of Jerusalem gathered on the Sabbath. There, the entire community would greet the various men who were about to be married in the coming week (Goldin, 1956).

Before the bride-to-be left her father's home on the wedding day, she would veil her face, which according to the Mishnah marked the social transition from girlhood to womanhood (Kethuboth ii, 1 and 10, referred to in Bader, 1988). The custom of covering the face is found in the story of Rebekah, who when she saw Isaac coming toward her, she grabbed a veil and covered her face. The term צעיף – *tsaiyph* – is the word translated "veil" (Genesis 24:65).

A later tradition emerged in the Middle Ages known as בדיכן – *badekenn* – the veiling ceremony, where the groom (on the wedding day) would walk up to the bride-to-be, and gently place the veil on her face. Greenburg suggested its origin stems from Jacob thinking he married Rachel but instead was married to Leah hidden by her veil (Greenberg, 1989). The family and friends of the bride and groom would then accompany the couple to the wedding canopy. At the actual time when the couple pledged their troth one to another, the bridegroom would remove the veil from the

Rebecca Meets Isaac
by James Tissot, c.1902
The Jewish Museum

bride's head and throw it on his own shoulder signifying thereby that he had taken upon himself the responsibility of the bride as head of his house. Vows would be exchanged, rings given, and a cup of wine shared by the couple (Khodadad, 1926). Harris, not seeing a formal religious ceremony spelled out in the Bible, wrongly concluded that there was no ceremony connected to the ancient marriage ritual (Harris, 1980). The cup Khodadad identified was the fourth cup in the ancient wedding ritual, with the first three occurring during the betrothal ceremony.

The event would be kicked off by the friends of the groom who would come by night to collect the bride-to-be and her family and escort them to the home of the groom-to-be.

This was the precursor of the modern wedding procession (Harris, 1980). John the Baptist portrays himself as the friend of the bridegroom (Jesus) and is quoted as saying, *He that hath the bride is the bridegroom: but the friend of the bridegroom, which standeth and heareth him, rejoiceth greatly because of the bridegroom's voice: this my joy therefore is fulfilled* (John 3:29). He concludes the passage with the famous expression, *He must increase, but I must decrease* (John 3.30).

A week-long celebration would then ensue with the consummation being performed the first night. The Ancient Arabs called the marriage celebration "saba" – "seven," because it extended over seven days (Morgenstern, 1966).

Jewish Wedding in Morocco
by Eugene Delacroix, c.1863
The Louvre
Wikimedia Commons

Among the ancient Jews, the tradition was that the groom was not permitted to leave the house of the bride's parents during the entire seven days. Entertainment was given each evening, continuing until daybreak (Benjamin, 1859).

The celebration had its origin in the scriptures. Jacob had celebrated his marriage to Leah for one week before he could take Rachel as his second wife (Genesis 29:27). In the period of the Judges, Sampson had a seven day feast when he took a wife from the Philistines (Judges 14:10-15). It should not be overlooked as to the significance of the number seven in Jewish numerology. Many consider it to be the number of completion based upon the story of creation in the opening book of the Bible.

The Jewish mystics found meaning in the ten pri mordial numbers and associated each with a category of creation. The numbers are called *sefiroth*. Seven corresponds to seven heavens, seven days of the week, seven orifices of the body and, in their perspective, the seven fundamental opposites in man's life: life and death, peace and disaster, wisdom and folly, wealth and poverty, charm and ugliness, sowing and devastation, domination and servitude (Scholem, 1987).

CHAPTER FIVE

JEWISH CUSTOMS ASSOCIATED WITH BETROTHAL AND MARRIAGE

The Jewish calendar has dictated certain periods of time that are either favorable or prohibitive towards marriage ceremonies. During the period between Pesach and Shavuot, marriages are not performed. This period of time is called the period of the counting the עמר – *omer* – literally "a heap" and describes a dry measure (Lev 23: 10-21). Orthodox Jews suggest that this ban on marriages commemorates the Hadrianic persecutions of Palestinian Jews in 125 A.D. There is an exception to this ban and on Lag B'Omer, the 33rd day of counting the Omer, the ban is lifted. This has become a popular day for weddings and commemorates the day that the persecutions ceased under Emperor Hadrian (Goldin, 1956).

The ninth day of the Hebrew month Av, known as Tisha B'Av, is another solemn date on the Jewish calendar. It is the date on which both the first and second Temples were destroyed in Jerusalem (586 B.C. by the Babylonians and 70 A.D. by the Romans). Weddings are banned for three weeks leading up to this date. Sabbaths, feast days, and days of fasting round out the forbidden days for weddings (Goldin, 1956, Greenberg, 1989). Tuesday (the third day of the week) is the preferred day on which to hold a wedding ceremony because it was twice blessed by God during creation (Genesis 1:10,12).

For many centuries the Jewish communities around the world held in high regard the persons that functioned as "matchmakers". The position was known in the Yiddish language as the שדכן – *shadchan.* Since the turn of the 20th Century when Sholem Aleichem wrote about Jewish life in Russia, the matchmaker has been immortalized in books, plays, and movies, most notably *Fiddler on the Roof.* The *Shadchan* is still respected among the Chasidic and more

The Matchmaker
by Gerard van Honthorst, c.1625
Centraal Museum, Utrecht/Ernst Moritz

Orthodox Jews around the world, but their techniques are evolving. Their service is now more akin to a good computer dating service (Greenberg, 1989).

The practice of child marriages ended in 1950, when the chief rabbinate of the State of Israel declared the minimum legal age for marriage to be sixteen (Klein, 1979). Prior to this edict, child marriages had to occur within the boundaries of what was known as "legal capacity". A minor, described as a male younger than 13 and a female younger than 12, was not allowed to become engaged or enter into marriage

unless they were orphaned. The girl would be legally able
to commit to a marriage at the age of 12½ years and one
day (Encyclopedia Judaica, Vol. 11, p 1050). The 1950 edict
was amended in 1960 to declare that a man could not legally
marry a woman younger than 17. There are provisions for
exceptions, but this remains the current practice in Israel.
Greenburg suggests that arranged marriages exist in the
present generation of Jews only among the most traditional
Jews, with the remainder of the Jews allowing the children to
select their own mates (Greenberg, 1989).

Khodadad suggested that a new bride had to become
an integral member of the bridegroom's clan. Because her
suitability was the concern of the whole family, the choice of a
suitable wife for a son was the recognized prerogative of the
head of the family (Khodadad, 1926).

Edersheim writes that in the background of every Jewish
marriage ceremony is the awareness of how it represents the
marriage between God and Israel. Indeed, Israel is called a
bride no less than ten times in the Old Testament (six times
in the Song of Songs, three times in Isaiah, and once in
Jeremiah) (Edersheim, 1883).

Jerusalem has a unique place in the heart of God.
The prophet Ezekiel speaking for the Lord described the
city as an infant whom the Lord observed when it was a
newborn with its navel uncut. It was unloved, unswaddled,
and uncared for. He described it as having been *cast out in
the open field* (Ezekiel 16: 5). As the city matured the Lord
saw it as a thing of beauty. It was a time for love and God
spread his skirt over it and declared that *thou becamest mine*
(Ezekiel 16:8). The term translated "*skirt*" is the Hebrew word
כנף – *kanaph* – which refers to a wing or corner of a garment
(Strong's word, 3671). The Mosaic law required every Jewish

male to tie fringes on each corner or wing of their garments
(Deuteronomy 15:37-41). He would hold these fringes,
known as *tzit tzit*, in his hands as he covered his head with
the garment for prayer. This would later become the prayer
shawl or *Tallit*. Fringes would also be tied on the canopy over
the marriage ceremony or *hupah*. The tradition has emerged
in Orthodox Jewish circles for the groom to bring his bride
under his *Tallit* during the wedding ceremony. The Lord's
spreading His skirt over Jerusalem may be the catalyst for
this tradition.

A New Testament example of God's selection of
Jerusalem as His bride is seen in chapter twenty-one of the
book of Revelation. An angel spoke to John and told him
to, *Come hither, I will show thee the bride, the Lamb's wife*
(Revelation 21:9). What he was shown was described as,
*that great city, the holy Jerusalem, descending out of heaven
from God* (Revelation 21:10).

In a prophetic mode, Isaiah spoke concerning
Jerusalem, decreeing that she will be a, *crown of joy and a
royal diadem...thou shalt be called Hephzibah* (name means
"my delight," Strong's word, 2657) *and thy land Beulah* (name
means "husband or master" and is the same root as Strong's
word, 1166 – בעל): *for the Lord delighteth in thee, and thy
land shall be married* (Isaiah 62:3-4). Harris, describing the
term "Beulah" as the passive participle of *baal*, suggests that
it signifies both the intimacy and the joy that the Lord has
in conjunction with Jerusalem and the entire land of Israel
(Harris, 1980).

The Jewish wedding tradition has included in its
ceremony an attempt to remember the plight of Jerusalem,
and always has recited during the ceremony the passage

from Psalm 137:5-6 where it states, *If I forget thee, O Jerusalem, let my right hand forget her cunning. If I do not remember thee, let my tongue cleave to the roof of my mouth; if I prefer not Jerusalem above my chief joy.*

The Four Cups
Jennifer Rigsby, Photographer, 2012
Courageous Fine Art

CHAPTER SIX

BETROTHAL METAPHOR IN THE PASSOVER

It was in the Exodus story that the courtship between God and the people of Israel was cemented. It was an event that would be referenced more than a hundred times in the scriptures. It was so significant an event for the people of Israel that God changed their calendars to make the month it was commemorated the beginning of their liturgical calendar (Exodus 12:2). It was an event of epic proportions, etched into the Jewish psyche, and it came with ten miracles (the plagues) and four promises.

The annual feast commemorating the Exodus is called פסח – *Pesach* or Passover. It is a marvelous commemorative feast, yet its importance transcends that of celebration. It is more than a holiday season. It is above all else, a memorial of freedom. With the event of the Exodus, Almighty God transformed a nomadic band of slaves into a nation that He could covenant to himself. God would hallow the date by commanding that Jews in every generation would observe the sanctity of it (Exodus 12:14, Leviticus 23:4-8).

The annual commemoration of Passover begins at sundown on the fourteenth day of the Hebrew month of Nisan. The Jewish celebration, which is the oldest continuously observed religious festival in the world (nearly 3500 years), begins around a dinner table. Traditions have long been developed with regard to both ceremonial and non-ceremonial food items to be eaten, amounts of wine to be imbibed, stories and songs to be shared, and ritual washings to be observed. The meal is called a סדר – *Seder* – meaning "order". No matter where one journeys in the world, and no matter what language one speaks, to attend a Jewish Seder on the 14th of Nisan would offer the opportunity to retell the story in solidarity with Jews around the world. This is accomplished by the tradition of following the order established in a booklet called a הגדה – *Haggadah* – which means "telling." It comprises a set form of benedictions, prayers, midrashic comments and psalms arranged in a precise outline. It is essentially an account of the story of Egyptian bondage, a thanksgiving to God for his redemption of Israel, and a prayer looking toward future redemption (Encyclopedia Judaica, Vol. 7, p.1079).

Israel in Egypt
by Sir Edward John Poynter, c.1867
Guildhall Art Gallery, London, UK
Wikimedia Commons

The Haggadah was initially transmitted from father to son, from family to family, and from generation to generation by word of mouth. However, it has been a codified tradition since the period of the "Men of the Great Assembly" circa 300 B.C. (Hacohen, 1987).

One of the distinct features of the order of service at a *Seder* involves the drinking of four cups of wine. Much debate by renowned Jewish sages of old offered a variety of explanations as to what the four cups represented. Some saw the significance of the number four linked with the S*eder*. There are four cups, four questions asked in the liturgy of that night, four symbolic foods eaten, and four sons mentioned. Other scholars observed that four times in the Torah it mentions the cup of Pharaoh. There were four evil decrees made by Pharaoh, and a few sages saw a parallel in that there have been four nations that have enslaved the Jews (Chaldeans, Medes, Greeks, and Romans). The debate was finally settled by the Jerusalem Talmud, which originated in the school of Johanan ben Nappaha of Tiberius (the Talmud is a collection of rabbinic notes on the oral tradition of the 2nd Century A.D. or of the Common Era as the Jews would prefer to say it). Rabbi Johanan quoted an earlier rabbi by the name of Benaiah by stating that the four cups represented the four expressions of divine redemption found in the Exodus story (Hacohen, 1987).

It should be noted that even the most cursory examination of the names associated with the four cups of wine imbibed at the Passover would produce dozens of names. There seems to be no agreement to their nomenclature within either Jewish or Christian scholarship. This author has preferred to link the name of each cup with the root concept of the promise they commemorate.

The first promise is recorded in chapter six of the book of Exodus. Verse six records these words, "Wherefore say unto the children of Israel, I am the Lord, and I will bring you out from under the burdens of the Egyptians…". The Hebrew word translated "bring" is the word יצא – yatsa – meaning- break out, bring forth, or carry out (Strong's word, 3318). It is the first cup partaken of at the meal and therefore has the distinction of being called the "Cup of Sanctification". The Hebrew word for sanctify is the word קדש- kadesh – which literally means to set apart or consecrate. This cup reminds the Jews of the blood that was applied to the doorposts and

The Signs on the Door
by James Tissot, c. 1896
The Jewish Museum

lintel of the Israelite homes in Egypt. The blood set them apart from the Egyptians and when the death angel saw the blood, he passed over their homes for they were consecrated and set apart for the Lord (Exodus 12: 21-28).

The second cup of wine at a *Seder* meal is called the "Cup of Salvation". The cup represents God's second promise to the Israelites, which stated that he would, "rid you out of their bondage" (Exodus 6:6). The root word for rid is the Hebrew word נצל – natsal – which means "to snatch away, save, rescue, deliver, etc." (Strong's word, 5337). Emphasis is placed on the aspect of snatching away or separating. God separated Israel from the Egyptians with the Exodus and later the gentile nations around them. History is a continuous testimony of how God has saved, rescued and delivered his people. One needs only to list the numerous cultures that have faded into history, yet Israel remains.

The Exodus Panorama
by James Tissot, c.1896-1902
The Jewish Museum

The Jewish world partakes of the second cup remembering how God delivered them from bondage. Not just the Israelites of old, but Jews in every generation are commanded to regard themselves as having been personally delivered. The scriptures commands: *show thy son in that day, saying, this is done because of that which the Lord did unto me when I came forth out of Egypt* (Exodus 13:8).

The Jews' Passover
by James Tissot, c.1896
The Jewish Museum

    The third cup of wine at a Passover *Seder* is called the "Cup of Redemption". It recalls God's third promise to Moses: *I will redeem you with a stretched-out arm, and with great judgments* (Exodus 6:6). The word redeem in this verse is used 118 times in the scriptures. It is the Hebrew word גאל – gaal – meaning "redeem, ransom, or purchase" (Strong's word, 1350). In the Oriental view of the law of kinship, it emphasizes redemption as being the privilege or duty of a near relative. God had commanded Moses to tell Pharaoh, *Israel is my son, even my first born* (Exodus 4:22). The privilege and responsibility to redeem Israel was God's alone. Jesus literally fulfilled this promise as He hung with stretched out arms on the cross.

The fourth cup of wine at a *Seder* is called the "Cup of Deliverance". It refers to God's fourth promise to Moses: *I will take you to me for a people* (Exodus 6:7). The Hebrew word translated take is the word לקח – laqach - whose meaning is to" take, receive or fetch" (Strong's word, 3947). In the scriptures there are two uses of the term where it describes bodily assumption into heaven. Reference is made of Enoch's disappearance when God *took him* (Gen. 5:25), and Elijah's assumption in a whirlwind (II Kings 2:3, 10-11).

Each of the four promises commemorated by these four cups of wine are replete with marriage covenant terminology. Hebrew translations allow the reader to more clearly understand the import of the promises. Consider how יצא – yatsa – means "carry out", נצל – natsal – means to "snatch away", גאל – gaal – means "purchase", and לקח – laqach – is used in the promise "I will take you to me for a people". This is the classical imagery of a knight in shinning armor taking or rescuing the woman he loves and making her his own. It is the way every man should feel toward his beloved. Although this author would never express it this way in front of his in-laws, he has always felt that he rescued his wife from her clan when he "took her" as his wife.

The Last Supper
by Charles Fairfax Murray in Stained Glass.
Located: Christ Church, Oxford, England

Chapter Seven

THE LAST SUPPER
AND BETROTHAL

All four of the New Testament Gospels present the story of the final celebration of a Passover *Seder* in which Jesus participated. It occurred on the last evening before His crucifixion. Matthew identifies the event as having occurred on *the first day of the feast of unleavened bread* (Matt. 26:17). Mark adds the caveat that it was the day that *they killed the Passover* (Mark 14:12). Luke writes, *Then came the day of unleavened bread, when the Passover must be killed* (Luke 22:7). John seems to contradict the three synoptic writers by indicating that the event was *before the feast of Passover, when Jesus knew that his hour was come that he should depart out of this world unto the Father* (John 13:1). Edersheim suggests it is almost impossible to imagine anything more evident, than that the scriptures are intended to have us understand that Jesus was about to celebrate the ordinary Jewish Paschal supper (Edersheim, 1886). He defers to a Jewish writer by the name of Joel Blicke (author of *Religionsgescichte zu Anfang des zweiten christlichen Jahrhunderts*) who, as one opposed to the notion of Jesus being the Messiah, determined that Jesus was crucified on the first Paschal day, and that this was only later modified to the eve of the "*Pascha*" (Blicke, referred to by Edersheim, 1886).

When it was time to sit down with His disciples to share in the traditional Passover *Seder* meal, Jesus told them, *With desire I have desired to eat this Passover with you before I suffer: For I say unto you, I will not any more eat thereof, until it be fulfilled in the kingdom of God* (Luke 22:15-16). It would be the Lord's last opportunity to address His disciples before His death. It would prove to be an evening of profound dialogue. The institution of the New Covenant and the establishment of the ordinance or sacrament of communion are events with which most Christians are familiar. However, few have examined the dialogue in the context of the meta-narrative of betrothal.

The Last Supper
by James Tissot, c.1890
Brooklyn Museum

Because the liturgy of the *Seder* meals had been codified in the generations that proceeded Jesus' time, the events recorded in the Upper Room can be placed within the context of the prescribed order. There would be benedictions, ritual washings, ceremonial foods, and the four cups of wine; two served before the meal and two after the meal.

Matthew and Mark both begin the narrative as Jesus and the disciples were eating with the declaration that one of the twelve would betray him (Matthew 26:20-21, Mark 14:17-18). Luke begins with the expression of how Jesus had desired to eat the meal with them before He would suffer, but immediately describes the self-imposed moratorium Jesus declared concerning His not eating of the Passover again or partaking of the fruit of the vine (wine) until *the kingdom of God shall come* (Luke 22:15-18). John picks up the narrative after the supper was ended, when Jesus arose from the table to wash His disciples' feet (John 13: 2-4). Like four gemologists viewing the same diamond from various angles, the gospel narrators provide four different glimpses of the drama that unfolded in the Upper Room that night.

The location of the event is not without controversy but is generally accepted to have occurred in the area of what today is called the Upper Room, Cenacle or the "coenaculum." This is the area which is today mistakenly called Mount Zion and is located outside the Zion gate of the Old City (Shanks, 1995). The term "Cenacle" comes from the Latin word *cena* meaning "dinner." The term "coenaculum" stems from the Latin *coena* which was the term for the eating room of the typical Roman house. It was usually located on an upper story and could be reached by an external staircase. The current room visited by pilgrims to the Holy Land is of later origin but may have been constructed upon the site of the original edifice.

As Jesus began to address the issue of betrayal, He identified the individual as being the one that *dippeth his hand with me in the dish* (Matthew 26:23). In the ancient order of service, such an opportunity would have occurred at the point of the ceremony known as the כורך – *korech* – which means "combine" and refers to the practice of combining the symbolic foods eaten at the *Seder*. These items included the lamb, matzah (unleavened bread), bitter herbs, and spring greens. The practice refers to the commandment found in Exodus 12:8 which states, *And they shall eat the flesh in that night, roast with fire, and unleavened bread; and with bitter herbs they shall eat it.* In John's Gospel it is referred to as a "sop" (John 13:26). The word sop is the Greek word ψωμίον – *psomeeon* – meaning "a mouthful" (Strong's word, 5596). The *korech* or sop would be combined and then fed to the person to one's left. The practice was cemented into the liturgy of the *Seder* in the time of Rabbi Hillel, who lived in the generation prior to Jesus (Edersheim, 1883).

Communion of the Apostles
aka *The Institution of the Eucharist*
by Joos van Wassenhove, c.1470
Galleria Nazionale delle Marche, Urbino, Italy

Jewish tradition directed that every participant reclined at the *Seder* meal on pillows; reclining on the left side in order to eat with the right hand. Edersheim suggested that this tidbit of information was an actual clue to the location of at least two of the disciples that night. John's Gospel speaks of John *lying on Jesus' breast.* This would indicate a position to the right of Jesus. With all reclining left this would put John's head in position to rest on the chest of the Lord. Combining the elements into a sop and feeding it to the person to the left would indicate that Judas Iscariot was located to his left (Edersheim, 1883, p 494).

When Jesus took the bread and blessed it, He would have done so in accordance with the liturgy long established for the *Seder.* The bread was unleavened as prescribed in the Exodus narrative and recalled the fact that the Israelites had to eat in such haste the day they departed Egypt that they did not have time for the bread to rise (Exodus 12:11). The traditional blessing is called the מצות מצה – *motzi matzah* – and would have included the words:

ברוך אתה יי אלהינו מלך העולם המוציא לחם מן־הארץ

Baruch atah Adonai, Elohenu melech haolam, hamotzi lechem min haaretz.

The traditional translation would read, "*Blessed art thou, Oh Lord our God, King of the universe, who brings forth bread from the earth.*"

Likewise, when Jesus lifted the cup of wine, the scripture states that He, *gave thanks* (Matthew 26:27). His blessing over the cup, if the traditional prescribed benediction was followed, would have been:

ברוך אתה יי אלהינו מלך העולם בורא פרי הגפן

Baruch atah Adonai Elohenu melech haolam, boree pre hagafin.

The traditional translation would read, *"Blessed art thou, Oh Lord our God, King of the universe, creator of the fruit of the vine"*.

The self-imposed moratorium on taking any further bread or wine is recorded in each of the synoptic texts. The question bodes itself, at which point was the moratorium imposed? Was it at the beginning of the evening or did it occur midway through the liturgy? A closer examination reveals that in Matthew and Mark the narratives record that it occurred *as they were eating* and *as they did eat* (Matthew 26:26, Mark 14:22). Yet, the event had to occur after Jesus dipped the sop (which included unleavened bread). Luke's text is less clear on this and would suggest that Jesus either began the evening with the fast or, by the English translation, implied He would not eat another *Seder* meal until *it be fulfilled in the kingdom of God* (Luke 22:16). Luke recorded the ban on drinking the wine, not as some ethereal future ban, but as an immediate act. He states, *I say unto you, I will not drink of the fruit of the vine, until the kingdom of God shall come* (Luke 2:18).

The timing crystallizes as the examination of the four cups of Jesus' last *Seder* is performed. The established liturgy called for two cups of wine to be imbibed before the meal and two cups served after the meal. Although Luke's account is less specific, Matthew and Mark suggest that the cup after the meal should be understood. The Apostle Paul certainly understood it this way and used the expression, τό ποτήριον μετά τό δειπνησαι – which translates as "the cup after the supper" for the timing for the institution of the New Testament (I Corinthians 11:25).

Although Luke would briefly comment on three additional themes (Judas the betrayer, the debate as to which disciple would be the greatest, and Peter's denial), it is John's Gospel that records the bulk of the material known in the Christian world as the "Upper Room Discourse."

Matthew and Mark record the singing of a hymn before the disciples followed Jesus to the Mount of Olives (Matthew 26:30, Mark 14:26). Edersheim identifies the hymn as the later portion of the הלל – *Hallel*, which is comprised of Psalms 115-118 (Edersheim, 1883). More accurately, it is the הלל מצרי – *Hallel Mizri* – Egyptian Hallel, which was chanted "antiphonally" or responsively in two parts by the time of the Talmud and probably much earlier. Yemenite Jews still respond with "*Hallelujah*" after each half of a verse, with European Jews (known as Ashkenazi Jews) repeating certain verses on cue (Encyclopedia Judaica, Vol. 7, p.1198). Greenberg states that Psalm 115 and 116 were sung before the meal and just prior to telling the story of the Passover, which is the portion known as the מגיד – *maggid* (Greenberg, 1989). That would leave Psalms 117 and 118 to be sung at the conclusion of the *Seder*.

Psalm 117 is only two verses long and speaks of how the truth of the Lord endures forever. Psalm 118 is much longer. The first four verses repeat the expression, *his mercy endureth forever*. The term mercy is the Hebrew word חסד – *chesed* – which often is translated "loving kindness, favour, or kindness" (Strong's word, 2617). Of the hundreds of times the word is used in the scriptures, it is nearly always closely placed with the Hebrew words, אמת or אמונה – *truth or faithfulness*. Farris, after careful analogy of each of the uses of the word translated "mercy," suggested that a more appropriate interpretation would be the expression, "covenant loyalty" as a covenant between a man and a woman requires fidelity, loyalty, and favor (Farris, 1981).

There are two additional verses in Psalm 118 of particular interest. The first is verse 22 which states, *the stone which the builders refused is become the headstone of the corner.* ראש פנה – *rosh pina* – the headstone was a reference back to the rebuilding of the Temple by Ezra more than five hundred years before Jesus. At the event of laying that headstone, the people celebrated, and sang the following praises to God, *for his mercy endureth for ever toward Israel* (Ezra 3:11). Each of the synoptic Gospels quotes the verse from Psalm 118:22. The Apostle Peter would use the metaphor of Jesus being the stone that was rejected by the Jewish leadership, but had become the head of the corner for salvation. He would conclude in the following verse that, *neither is there salvation in any other: for there is none other name under heaven given among men, whereby we must be saved* (Acts 4:11-12). When Paul was declaring the unity of all believers through Jesus' sacrifice on the cross, he wrote that gentiles who believed in Jesus were now fellow citizens with the Jews and no more alienated from them, having been built upon the foundation of the Apostles and Prophets, *Jesus Christ himself being the chief corner stone; in whom all the building fitly framed together growth unto a holy temple in the Lord; in whom ye also are builded together for a habitation of God through the Spirit* (Ephesians 2:11-22).

It is interesting to note that at the model of the Second Temple Period Jerusalem (now located near the Shrine of the Book in Jerusalem), there is a noticeable rock formation that can be seen outside of what was then the western gate of the city walls surrounding Jerusalem of Herod's day. It was the location of what became a rather large quarry from which many hewn blocks were cut and used in the construction of Herod's numerous projects in the city, including the Temple and the complex surrounding it. The formation that protrudes above the surrounding quarry site was the place of stoning and later crucifixion. Today that rock is located under the Church of the Holy Sepulcher. Two decades after Jesus, the city wall on the north was pushed further out resulting in the area of the quarry now being included within the city walls (Shanks, 1995). The stone that protruded had too many fishers in it to be viable for the masons to use. It had literally been rejected stone and fulfilled Isaiah's prophecy, ... *Behold, I lay in Zion for a foundation a stone, a tried stone, a precious corner stone, a sure foundation* ... (Isaiah 28:16). The Hebrew word translated "tried" is the word בחן – *bochan*, whose root means "to test, to examine, or prove" (Strong's word, 976). The stone masons had tested the rock formation and rejected it. Jesus, too, was tested by Satan, examined by the Jewish leadership, tried by Pilot, and proven worthy by His sacrifice.

The other verse from Psalm 118 that cannot be overlooked is verse 26 which states, *Blessed be he that cometh in the name of the Lord: we have blessed you out of the house of the Lord.* The first portion of the verse is translated from the Hebrew expression ברוך הבא בשם יהוה – *baruch haba bashem Adonai.* It is the exact expression that is spoken as the groom is invited under the wedding *chuppah* in the wedding ceremony (Golden, 1956). It should not be overlooked that as Jesus made His triumphal entry into the city of Jerusalem only days before His death, crowds that formed cried out to Him saying, *Hosanna to the Son of David: Blessed is he that cometh in the name of the Lord: Hosanna in the highest* (Matthew 21:9). Keil and Delitzsch suggested that this expression would be reserved for the "longed-for guest of the feast" (Keil & Delitzsch, 1986, Vol. 5, p. 231). Jesus would Himself intone the same words as He wept over the city of Jerusalem. Matthew records Jesus as saying, *For I say unto you, Ye shall not see me henceforth, till ye shall say, Blessed is he that cometh in the name of the Lord* (Matthew 23:39). Luke, addressing the same event, added

Palm Sunday Procession on the Mount of Olives
by James Tissot, c.1896
Brooklyn Museum

that those people present *knewest not the time of thy visitation* (Luke 19:44). Their eyes were blinded, and they missed the importance of what Jesus was saying.

The Apostle John wrote five chapters on the events that took place in the Upper Room following the supper. He begins by describing the act of Jesus washing the disciples'

feet. There had already been two specific ritual washings of
the hands during the *Seder* liturgy. These events were known
as ורחץ – *urechatz*. Hands are washed in accordance with
the ancient practice of ritual purification before partaking
of anything dipped in a liquid. Buxbaum suggests that as
the water pours over the hands, a person should abase
themselves of lower self-concerns and desires, and as hands
are then lifted from the water thoughts should turn to the holy
intentions for eating the meal (Buxbaum, 1990). Edersheim
suggested that Jesus' washing of the disciples' feet must
have occurred during the first of the two ritual washings
(Edersheim, 1883). This would be in direct conflict with
John 13:2, which specifically mentions that the foot washing
occurred after the meal.

Of peculiar interest are the statements Jesus made
with reference to washing. He first mentioned that, *What
I do thou knowest not now; but thou shalt know hereafter*
(John 13:7). Plummer suggested that the disciples would
not learn the meaning of these words until Pentecost – 51
days later (Plummer, 1981). Morris points out that this type
of ritual washing was not required of a Hebrew slave but was
obligatory for a spouse (Morris, 1971). Jesus then told the
disciples that, *If I wash thee not, thou hast no part with me*
(John 13:8). This was followed by Peter's acquiescence and
submission for the ceremonial rite. Jesus then said, *he that
is washed needeth not save to wash his feet, but is clean
every whit: and ye are clean...* (John 13:10). This would
be reinforced two chapters later when Jesus would declare
the disciples to be, *clean through the word which I have
spoken unto you* (John 15:3). It has already been shown
that a ritual washing was crucial in the bride's preparation
before the ancient nuptials would be exchanged. It signaled

the transition from the single life to the life of matrimonial covenant.

The language used in the Upper Room Discourse was filled with language commonly used in the marriage covenant. Just as the groom-to-be in the ancient ritual would have promised his betrothed that he would prepare the home and return, Jesus declared, *In my Father's house are many mansions: if it were not so I would have told you. I go to prepare a place for you and if I go and prepare a place for you, I will come again, and receive you unto myself; that where I am, there ye may be also* (John 14:2-3).

Ancient Ruins at Capernaum
Author's Archive

Excavations in various places around Israel reveal that houses in the second Temple period typically involved the son building on to his parents' existing dwelling. Over time this produced a labyrinth of buildings difficult to sort out. The common house in Capernaum, for example, had many roofed rooms around a common courtyard and was shared by kindred families living in a patriarchal community (Loffreda, 2001).

In the ancient betrothal ceremony, the needs of the bride-to-be were transferred from her father's responsibility to the family of the groom-to-be. In the Upper Room, Jesus promised the disciples that *If ye shall ask any thing in my name, I will do it* (John 14:14). This would be repeated in chapter 15:7, *If ye abide in me, and my words abide in you, you shall ask what ye will, and it shall be done unto you*, and in chapter 16:23-24, *And in that day you shall ask me nothing. Verily, Verily, I say unto you, whatsoever ye shall ask the Father in my name, he will give it you. Hitherto have ye asked nothing in my name: ask, and ye shall receive, that your joy may be full.*

The betrothal ritual involved the groom-to-be giving his betrothed gifts. In the Upper Room, Jesus promised the gift of the Holy Spirit with the words, *If ye love me, keep my commandments. And I will pray the Father, and he shall give you another Comforter, that he may abide with you forever* (John 14:17).

The groom-to-be would promise to return for his bride at a future date. Jesus is recorded as stating, *I will not leave you comfortless: I will come to you* (John 14:18). This would be reiterated four verses later as Jesus declared, *If a man love me, he will keep my words: and my Father will love him, and we will come unto him, and make our abode with him* (John 14:23). The word "abode" comes from the Greek word μονή – *mone* – meaning "residence or mansion" (Strong's word, 3438).

The word "love" is used in John's account in the Upper Room narrative sixteen times. Nearly all of them using the

Greek ἀγπη – *agape* – which speaks of "seeking the higher good of the one loved" (Strong's word, 26). The bride would expect nothing less from her groom.

Having sung the Hallel as a hymn, the gospel timeline of the last evening events states that the disciples went to the Mount of Olives (Matthew 26:30, Mark 14: 26, Luke 22:39, John 18:1). John's Gospel adds that, *Jesus ofttimes resorted thither with his disciples* (John 18:2). The location was the ancient olive press known as Gethsemane. Its name comes from the Aramaic term for oil press. The traditional site, which today has the Church of all Nations on the property and adjacent to which is a plot of land with some of the oldest olive trees to be found in the Holy Land, is not without dispute. The Roman Catholics have dominated the traditional location since the Byzantine Era (the present edifice built upon the ruins of an earlier Byzantine structure), but the Greek Orthodox Church has their own location further up the Mount of Olives. Thomson and others suggest neither is accurate, suggesting a position several hundred yards northeast of the present church (Unger, 1974; Thomson, 1858).

Regardless of the original location, the actual events that are recorded in the gospel narratives were profound. Matthew records that three times Jesus prayed concerning *the cup*. In the first prayer, Matthew records Jesus words as, *O my Father, if it be possible, let this cup pass from me: nevertheless not as I will, but as thou wilt* (Matthew 26:39). In the second prayer, Jesus stated, *O my Father, if this cup may not pass away from me, except I drink it, thy will be done* (Matthew 26:42). The third prayer is simply recorded as his *saying the same words* (Matthew 26:44). The term translated "prayed" is the Greek word προσεύχομαι – *proseuchomai*

– which speaks of earnest prayer. It comes from the root meaning "to worship" (Strong's word, 4336). Brown traced the word to the concept of bowing and blowing kisses before someone (Brown, 1976). The earnestness of his prayers is corroborated by the account recorded in Luke where Jesus' sweat became *great drops of blood* (Luke 22:44). The medical terminology for this is *hematidrosis*. It occurs when severe anxiety causes the release of chemicals that break down the capillaries in the sweat glands (Strobel, 1998).

The meta-narrative of betrothal in relation to the four cups would suggest that Jesus partook of the Cup of Sanctification at the Last Supper meal. The second cup (Cup of Salvation) corresponded to the negotiated price being determined. The Father would have been involved in this negotiation, but with whom? Was it with the prince of the power of the air? Was it with the one who held the keys to death and the grave? Theological debate could continue *ad infinitem.* Because the second cup was also partaken before the meal was served (by established *Seder* protocol) suggests that Jesus imbibed it with His disciples. Terms *tenaim* (or conditions) were established by God the Father and Jesus would be required to partake of the third cup (Cup of Redemption), before the betrothal to His bride could be in effect. It was this cup Jesus had agonized over in Gethsemane. It was this cup that Jesus had said He would not partake of until all things were fulfilled.

Judas Iscariot led a band of men and officers to the place with which he was familiar. He betrayed Jesus with a kiss on the cheek. Peter, who had brought with him a dagger, drew it out of its scabbard and wielded it at the High Priest's servant named Malcus (John 18:10). Luke records that Jesus touched Malcus' ear and healed him (Luke 22:51).

Jesus turned to Peter and made the statement, *Put up thy sword into the sheath: the cup which my Father hath given me, shall I not drink it?* (John 18:11).

The Healing of Malchus
by James Tissot, c.1896
Brooklyn Museum

This verse reinforces the concept that the Father had made the determination of the price Jesus would have to pay for His bride. The determined price would have been sealed with the second cup in the ancient betrothal ritual. Jesus was telling Peter that the third cup had been given to Him by the Father and that He would be required to drink it. It should not be overlooked that it was in Gethsemane that the decision was made to follow through with the arrangement.

Less than 24 hours after Jesus had issued the moratorium of the third cup, He was nailed to a cross. Matthew records that early in the crucifixion soldiers gave Jesus vinegar that was mingled with gall, but He would not drink it (Matthew 27:34). He had pronounced a moratorium of His drinking wine in the Upper Room. The word vinegar is a translation of the Greek word ὀξύς – *oxos* – which comes from a root expression meaning "keen, rapid, sharp, or swift" (Strong's word, 3691). Webster's Dictionary refers to vinegar as soured wine. It lists the origin of the word as coming from the French *vin* (wine) and *aigre* (keen, or sour): it is made from the fermentation of diluted alcoholic liquids.

The Wine Mixed with Myrrh
by James Tissot, c.1886-94
Brooklyn Museum

Gall is a translation of the Greek word χολή – *chole* – which was a substance with a greenish hue, used as an anodyne. In quantity, it was poison. Frequently, it was translated "wormwood, or poppy" (Strong's word, 5521).   In smaller quantity it was used to assuage pain. Webster's Dictionary identifies gall as "bile obtained from an animal which was used as medicine" (Webster, 1996). Mark's Gospel records the fluid offered to Jesus in this early attempt to medicate Him as being wine mingled with myrrh (Mark 15:23). This verse confirms that Jesus, indeed, did not partake of it. The Greek word for wine is οίνος – *oinos* – simply meaning "wine" (Strong's word, 3631). The word for myrrh in the Greek is σμυρνίζω – *smurnizo* – whose root means "to strengthen, as with a narcotic." It was bitter oil mixed with wine (Strong's word, 4669). Edersheim notes that it was a Jewish practice to offer the condemned a drink of strong wine that had been mixed with myrrh so as to "deaden consciousness." He describes a text from the Talmud that spoke of the practice and identified a women's association in Jerusalem which undertook this task as a ministry (Edersheim, 1883, p.590).

The events that occurred moments before Jesus expired on that fateful afternoon must be compiled from each of the gospel narratives. Matthew and Mark both describe Jesus' Aramaic pronouncement; *E'li, E'li, la'ma sa-bach'-tha-ni?* That is to say, *My God, my God, why hast thou forsaken me?* (Mathew 27: 46). Confusing this outburst as a cry to the prophet Elijah, someone took a sponge dipped in vinegar, and gave it to Him to drink. After receiving it, Matthew describes one more sigh *with a loud voice*, before Jesus expired (Matthew 27:50).

Luke describes the narrative between the thieves on the cross and then describes the darkness that fell *over all the earth* for three hours. He then described how the veil in the Temple was *rent in the midst*. Immediately, Jesus entrusted His spirit into His Father's hands and died (Luke 23:39-46). The word veil is translated from the Greek word καταπέτασμα – *katapetasma* – which is a composite word combining κατα – meaning "down", and πέτομαι – *petomai* – referring to "something spread thoroughly" (Strong's word, 2665). The

The Crucifixion
by Simon Vouet, c.1622
Church of Jesus, Genoa, Italy
Wikimedia Commons

parallel of the traditional בדיכן – *badeken – veil ceremony*, which is a tradition commemorating Jacob not knowing who he had married because she was veiled, should not be overlooked. The traditional orthodox interpretation of the veil representing the barrier that existed between God and man being rent so that we could now have access by faith is understood.

John describes the last moments as comprising Jesus making sure His mother would be cared for. Then, in an act to fulfill scripture, he describes Jesus as speaking the words,

I thirst (John 19:28). As with the gospel accounts of Matthew and Mark, John describes that someone took a sponge of hyssop, dipped it in vinegar (soured wine), and when Jesus had *received it*, He spoke the expression, *it is finished*, and He died (John 19:29-30).

The Rending of the Veil
by William Bell Scott, 1868
Wikimedia Commons

There begs the need to evaluate the veil in relation to the ancient veiling of the bride. This notion is poignantly addressed by the Apostle Paul, who when writing to the Hebrews, speaks of Jesus being the, *author and finisher of our faith; who for the joy that was set before him endured the cross...* (Hebrews 2:2). Was it the bride set before Him that brought Him joy on the cross? Could the veil being rent in the Temple symbolically represent the veil being removed so that Jesus could see His bride? This cannot be argued from the scripture, and scholarship has failed to address it adequately, but the notion has been proffered.

CHAPTER EIGHT

THE FOURTH CUP OF BETROTHAL AND MARRIAGE

John Eldredge in his book entitled <u>Wild at Heart</u> suggests that there are three things a man needs to feel successful in life. He lists them as, 1) an adventure to live, 2) a battle to fight, and 3) a damsel to rescue (Eldredge, 2001). Because man is fashioned in the likeness of God, one can assume that He himself had the same drives. Leaving His position in Heaven and taking the form of a man gave Him the adventure to live. His adversary gave Him the battle to fight and His nature (God is love) drove Him to rescue a damsel. That damsel was the nation of Israel. By His death on the cross, the barrier between Jew and Gentile has been removed through faith in Jesus, and we are *builded together for a habitation of God through the Spirit* (Ephesians 2: 14-22). Nothing and no one can ever come between the covenant of marriage established as betrothal on the cross. Betrothal has occurred for all who have embraced Jesus.

It bears repeating: the fourth cup is untouched; the marriage between Jesus and His bride is yet to come but already determined. When it does occur, it will not be a surprise for Jesus and His bride to drink from the fourth cup (Cup of Deliverance), after which Jesus will lay the cup on the earth and crush it with His foot.

And I heard as it were the voice of a great multitude, and as the voice of many waters, and as the voice of mighty thunderings, saying, Alleluia: for the Lord God omnipotent reigneth. Let us be glad and rejoice, and give honor to him: for the marriage of the Lamb is come, and His wife hath made herself ready. And to her was granted that she should be arrayed in fine linen, clean and white: for the fine linen is the righteousness of saints. And he saith unto me, write, Blessed are they which are called unto the marriage supper of the Lamb. And he saith unto me, These are the true sayings of God. (Revelation 19:6-9).

The meta-narrative of betrothal confirms the reality that God is not a helpless or hopeless romantic, but that He is simply an eternal romantic. He has sought out a people for Himself (Israel), He has wooed her, courted her, and betrothed her unto Himself. Even though she has proven unfaithful, His love has been unwavering. His purpose is to speak from His heart in their time of trouble and win back their affections. He has betrothed them unto Himself just as Hosea foretold.

It should be remembered that betrothal was a covenant that came with responsibilities that if breached had capital punishment consequences. The meta-narrative of betrothal links the Lord's Supper table to betrothal. Paul concluded his narrative to the Corinthians on this topic by issuing a warning. *Whosoever shall eat this bread, and drink this cup of the Lord, unworthily, shall be guilty of the body and blood of the Lord* (I Corinthians 11:27). Paul's exhortation was for those desiring to participate in the act to first examine themselves. He used the Greek word δοκιμάζω – *dokimazo* – for the word translated "*examine*". It means "to test, discern, or to prove" (Strong's word, 1381). In Paul's understanding, only those who proved worthy could partake of the elements and not incur judgment.

Paul declared that the unworthy participants would receive *damnation.* This is a strong expression of condemnation which comes from the Greek root word κρίνω – *krino* – "to distinguish or decide punishment" (Strong's word, 2919). Paul acknowledges that many have partaken unworthily and thus were now weak and sick, and that many have died for doing so (I Corinthians 11:30). His comments concerning the judgment of death are clear when equating the cup of communion with the betrothal cup.

One should pause prior to drinking from the communion cup and allow the Holy Spirit to whisper to the individual, *Will you go with this man?* By saying yes, the participant in communion is making a public declaration that their intention is to betroth themselves to Jesus. This makes the otherwise routine participation an act of renewal of betrothal vows. To partake and then to live a life contrary to a life of fidelity to God is a breach of the marriage covenant. Paul was stressing its importance when he issued such a serious warning. By renewing the vows in a faithful manner, the act is elevated to a spiritual level which mere words cannot sufficiently describe. How special it would be if every Christian fully appreciated where the communion table fit into the meta-narrative of betrothal and understood how near we are to the return of our Beloved. The parable of the ten virgins challenges us to be vigilant as we wait for the procession to begin.

Hopefully, you have paused long enough at a communion table to hear the Holy Spirit whisper in your ears those immortal words once spoken to Rebekah, *Will you go with this man?* She was found at a well drawing water for her flock. Abraham's servant had prayed that he would know her by her action at the well. Like Abraham, our Savior has come to find a bride. He is old fashioned but determined. Nothing can separate you from His love. The question left unanswered is *how will you respond at the well?*

> *The Spirit and the Bride say come. And let him that is athirst come. And whosoever will, let him take the water of life freely* (Revelation 22:17).

ABOUT THE MANUSCRIPT

Dr. Richard (Rick) M. Sharp first presented this manuscript as a lecture before the Oxford Graduate School Congregation in Tennessee the Spring of 2009. It was later presented as a lecture during the Oxford Scholar's Forum at Rewley House, University of Oxford, UK (January 2010). The codification was made for submission and advancement in the Oxford Society of Scholars.

BIBLIOGRAPHY

WORKS CITED

Bader, G. (1988). The encyclopedia of Talmudic sages. Northvale: Jason Aronson, Inc.

Benjamin, I.J. (1859). Eight years in Asia and Africa. London: Hanover.

Blomberg, C.L. (1997). Jesus and the gospels. Nashville: Broadman & Holman Publishers.

Beecroft, J., Rivington, J., White, B., (1771) Book of Common Prayer. Cambridge: John Archdeacon Printer.

Brown, C. (edt.) (1976). The new international dictionary of New Testament theology. Grand Rapids: Zondervan.

Buxbaum, Y. (1990). Jewish spiritual practices. Northvale: Jason Aronson Inc.

Cantarella, E. (1987). Pandora's daughters: The role and status of women in Greek and Roman antiquity. Baltimore: Johns Hopkins.

Cook, S.A. (1903). The laws of Moses and the code of Hammurabi. London: Adam and Charles Black.

Edersheim, A. (1883). The life and times of Jesus the Messiah. McLean: Macdonald Publishing House.

Eldredge, J. (2001). Wild at heart: Discovering the secret of a man's heart. Nashville: Thomas Nelson Publishing.

Encyclopedia Judaica. (1972). Vol: 5, subject Concubine. New York: Macmillan Company.

Encyclopedia Judaica. (1972). Vol: 7, subject Haggadah. New York: Macmillan Company.

Encyclopedia Judaica. (1972). Vol:11, subject Marriage. New York: Macmillan Company.

Epstein, L. (1927). The Jewish marriage contract. New York: Jewish Theological Seminary.

Farris, C. (1981). The Exodus. Memphis: Notes from course taught at Mid-America Baptist Theological Seminary.

Friedman, A.M. (1986). Marriage as an institution: Jewry under Islam.

Ganzfried, S. B. J. (1928). Code of Jewish law: A compilation of Jewish laws and customs. New York: Hebrew Publishers.

Ginzberg, H.L. (translator) (1969). Mibtahiah's first marriage: Aramaic papyri from Elephantine. Princeton: Princeton University Press.

Ginzberg (Ed.) (1964). Ishei ha-tanakh. New York: Shaar Press.

Golden, H.E. (1956). Hamadrikh – The rabbi's guide: A manuel of Jewish religious rituals, ceremonies, and customs. New York: Hebrew Publishing Company.

Greenberg, B. (1989). How to run a traditional Jewish household. London: Jason Aronson Inc.

Hacohen, M. & Ron, H. (1987). The Passover haggadah: Legends and customs. New York: Adama Books.

Hamon, R. R. & Ingoldsby B. B. (Ed.) (2004). Mate selection across cultures. London: Sage Publications.

Hapgood, I. F. (1975). Service book of the Holy Orthodox-Catholic Apostolic Church. Englewood: Antiochian Orthodox Christian Archdiocese.

Harris, R.L., Archer, G.L., and Waltke, B.K. (1980). Theological wordbook of the Old Testament. Chicago: Moody Press.

Hartman, L.F. (1963). Encyclopedic dictionary of the bible. New York: McGraw- Hill Book Company.

Harvey, D. (1989). The condition of postmodernity: An enquiry into the origins of cultural change. Cambridge: Blackwell.

Isaacson, B. (1979). Dictionary of the Jewish religion. Englewood: SBS Publishing.

Kaiser, W.C. (Ed.) (2005). NIV archeological study bible: An illustrated walk through biblical history and culture. Grand Rapids: Zondervan.

Keil, C.F. & Delitzsch, F. (1986). Commentary on the Old Testament in ten volumes: volume 1, the Pentateuch. Grand Rapids: William B. Eerdmans Publishing Company.

Keil, C.F. & Delitzsch, F. (1986). Commentary on the Old Testament in ten volumes: volume 5, the Psalms. Grand Rapids: William B. Eerdmans Publishing Company.

Khodadad, K. E. (1926). The social life of a Jew in the time of Christ. Liverpool; J.A. Thompson.

Klein, I. (1979). A guide to Jewish religious practice. New York: Jewish Theological Seminary of America.

Loffreda, S. (2001). Recovering Capharnaum. Jerusalem: Franciscan Printing Press.

Lyotard, J.F. (1979). The postmodern condition: A report on knowledge. Minneapolis: University of Minnesota Press.

McNeile, A.H. (1980). Thornapple commentaries: The gospel according to St. Matthew. Grand Rapids: Baker Book House.

Meyer, E. (1906). Die Israeliten und ihre nachbarstaemme. Leipzig: Halle Press.

Montgomery, J.A. (1934). Arabia and the bible. Philadelphia: University of Pennsylvania Press.

Morgenstern, J. (1966). The rites of birth, marriage, death, and kindred occasions among Semites. Cincinnati: Hebrew Union College Press.

Morris, L. (1971). The gospel according to John: The English text with introduction, exposition and notes. Grand Rapids: Eerdmans Publishing Co.

Nejat, N. & Rhea, K. (1998). Dailey life in ancient Mesopotamia. London: Greenwood Press.

New York Times, *Shaking off the shame*, November 26, 2009

Plummer, A. (1981). The gospel according to St. John. Grand Rapids: Baker Book House.

Pomeroy, S. (1975). Goddesses, whores, wives, and slaves: Women in classical antiquity. New York: Schoken.

Pritchard, J.B. (Ed.) (1969). Ancient near eastern texts relating to the Old Testament. Princeton: Princeton University Press.

Pritchard, J.B. (Ed.) (1987). The Harper atlas of the bible. New York: Harper & Row.

Richardson, M.E.J. (2000). Hammurabi's laws: Text, translation and glossary. Sheffield: Sheffield Academic Press.

Roth, M.T. (1995). Law collections from Mesopotamia and Asia Minor. Atlanta: Scholar's Press.

Schlesinger, B. (1987). Jewish family issues: A resource guide. New York: Garland.

Scholem, G. (1987). Origins of the Kabbalah. Princeton: The Jewish Publication Society.

Schram, P. (2000). Stories within stories from the Jewish oral tradition. Jerusalem: Jason Aronson Inc.

Scott, J. (1995). Customs and controversies: Intertestamental Jewish backgrounds of the New Testament. Grand Rapids: Baker Books

Shanks, H. (1995). Jerusalem: An archeological biography. New York: Random House.

Stone, E.C. (1982). The social role of the Naditu women in old Babylonian Nippur. Journal of the Economic and Social History of the Orient, V 25: p.55-56. Oxford: Brill Publications.

Strobel, L. (1998). The case for Christ: A journalist's personal investigation of the evidence for Jesus. Grand Rapids: Zondervan.

Strong, J. (1890). The exhaustive concordance of the bible: showing every word of the text of the common English version of the canonical books, and every occurrence of each word in regular order; together with dictionaries of the Hebrew and Greek words of the original, with references to the English words. Hendersonville: Mendenhall Sales, Inc.

The Holy Bible (KJV).

Thomson, W. M. (1858). Biblical illustrations drawn from the manners and customs, the scenes and scenery of the holy land. New York: Harper & Brothers.

Unger, M.F. (1974). Unger's bible dictionary. Chicago: Moody Press.

Webster, M. (1996). Merriam Webster's collegiate dictionary, tenth edition. Springfield: Merriam-Webster, Incorporated.

Weinreich, U. (1968). Modern English-Yiddish Yiddish-English Dictionary. New York: McGraw Hill.

West, S.S. (2000). Journey into the past: life in ancient Greece. London: The Reader's Digest Association Publisher.

Winton, T.D. (1958). Documents from old testament times. London: Thomas Nelson and Sons, Ltd.

Woolley, C.L. (1928). The Summerians. Oxford: Clarendon Press.

Woolley, C.L. (1936). Abraham: recent discoveries. London: Faber and Faber.

Woolley, C.L. (1954). Excavations at Ur. London: Earnest Benn Ltd.

Zuesse, E.M. (1987). Ritual, encyclopedia of religion, v.12, p405. New York: Macmillan Press.

BIBLIOGRAPHY

RELATED WORKS

Burder, S. (1808). Oriental customs: or an illustration of the
sacred scriptures, by an explanatory application of
the customs and manners of the eastern nations and
especially the Jews therein alluded to. Collected from the
most celebrated travelers, and the most eminent critics.
London: C. Whittingham, Goswell Street; for Longman,
Hurst, Rees, and Orme Paternoster Row.

Burrows, M. (1938). The basis of Israelite marriage. Ann Arbor:
The American Oriental Society.

Collings, J. S. (1928). The betrothal. London: British Broadcasting
Corporation.

Douce, F. (1814). Remarks on some ancient marriage customs.
London: Archaeologia, vol. xvii.

Epstein, L.M. (1942). Marriage Laws in the Bible and the Talmud.
Cambridge: Harvard University Press.

Friedlander, G. (1937). Laws and customs of Israel: compiled
from codes

Adam (Life of Man), kizzur shulchan aruch (condensed code of
laws): in four parts: dat va din: 'al-pi hayei adam ve-kitsur
shulchan 'arukh. London: Shapiro, Vallentine and Co.

Godwyn, T. (MDCLXVII). Moses and Aaron: civil and
ecclesiastical rites: used by the ancient Hebrews;
observed, and at large opened, for the clearing of many
obscure texts throughout the whole scripture, Which texts
are now added to the end of the book. Wherein likewise
is showed what customs the Hebrews borrowed from
heathen people: and that many heathenish customs,
originally, have been unwarrantable imitations of the
Hebrews. Ninth edition. London: S. Griffin.

Goodman, P., & Goodman, H. (1965). The Jewish marriage
anthology. New York: Jewish Publishing Company.

Hooke, S.H. (1938). The origins of early Semitic history, London: Oxford University Press.

Jacob, W. & Zemer, M. (1999). Marriage and its obstacles in Jewish law: essays and response. Tel Aviv: Freehof Institute of Progressive Halakhah.

Kahana, K. (1966). The theory of marriage in Jewish law. Boston: Brill.

Kertzer, D.I. (1988). Ritual, politics, and power. New Haven: Yale University Press.

Kruemer, D. (ed). (1986). The Jewish family metaphor and memory. New York: Oxford University Press.

Kuhrt, A. (1995). Ancient Mesopotamia in classical Greek and Hellenistic thought. New York: Cane.

Maude, M.F. (1849). Scripture manners and customs: being an account of the domestic habits, arts, etc., of eastern nations mentioned in holy scripture given principally in extracts from the works of travelers. London: Society for Promoting Christian Knowledge.

Miller, D. (1930). The secret of the Jew: his life - his family, a marriage guide – how to stay married, what a married daughter of Israel must know. Oakland: David Miller.

Neufeld, E. (1944). Ancient Hebrew marriage laws. London: Longman's.

Neusner, J. (2000). The Halakhah: an encyclopedia of the law of Judaism. Boston: Brill.

Orchard, D. B. (2001). The betrothal and marriage of Mary to Joseph: a spiritual meditation given to the London branch of the Society at Ealing Abbey, London on 2 February 2001. Wallington: Ecumenical Society of the Blessed Virgin Mary.

Picture Gallery. (1825). The picture gallery explored; or, an account of various ancient customs and manners. London: Harvey and Darton.

Rubin, N. (2008). Time and life cycle in Talmud and Midrash: socio-anthropological perspectives. Boston: Academic Studies Press.

Sanders, E.P. (1992). Judaism: practice and belief, 63 bce-66ce. Philadelphia: Trinity Press International.

Schlesinger, B. (ed). (1971). The Jewish family: a survey and annotated bibliography. Toronto: University of Toronto Press.

Swidler, L. (1979). Biblical affirmations of women. Philadelphia: Westminster.

Whitehouse, O.C. (1895). A primer of Hebrew antiquities. London: Religious Tract Society.

Wilson, M. R. (1989). Our father Abraham. Grand Rapids: Eerdmans.

FIGURES/ILLUSTRATIONS

1. *Abraham's Probable Route to the Holy Land:* Adam Clarke, c. 1832

2. *Abraham's Journey from Ur to Canaan* by Jozsef Molnar, c. 1850

3. *Excavated Street in the City of Ur* dated to 2100 B.C.,

4. *Code of Hammurabi* Stone Tablet, c. 1754 BCE
   Marie-Lan Nguyen, Photographer, 2006

5. *The Burial of Sarah* by Gustave Dore, c. 1866

6. *David Sees Bathsheba Bathing* by James Tissot, c. 1896-1902

7. *Abram's Counsel to Sarai* by James Tissot, c. 1896-1902

8. *Sarai Is Taken to Pharaoh's Palace* by James Tissot, c. 1896-1902

9. *Sarah Leading Hagar to Abraham* by Matthias Stom, c. 1639

10. *Abraham Dismissing Hagar and Ishmael* by Barent Fabritius,
    c. 1660

11. *Solomon and His Harem* by James Tissot, c.1870

12. *Rachel and Leah* by James Tissot, c. 1870

13. *The Rape of the Sabine Women* by Pietro da Cortona, c.1627

14. *Judah and Tamar* by Horace Vernet, c. 1840

15. *The Seduction of Dinah, Daughter of Leah* by James Tissot   ,
    c. 1896-1902

16. *Joseph and Potiphar's Wife* by Guido Reni, c. 1626

17. *Amnon and Tamar* by Jan Steen, c. 1650

18. *The Wedding of Samson* by Rembrandt van Rijn, c. 1638

19. *The Wedding at Cana* by Paolo Veronese, c. 1563

20. *The Unequal Marriage* by Vasily Pukirev, c. 1862

21. *Legal Document Dated to 139 A.D. on Vellum*, Author's Archive

22. *Jewish Headdress*, Jewish Virtual Library

23. *Wedding Procession, Jodhpur* by Edwin Lord Weeks, c. 1892

24. *Bedouin Woman with Her Dowry, c. 1900*

25. *Common Jewish Wedding Ring*, Author's Archive

26. *Rebecca and Eliezer at the Well* by Carlo Maratta, c. 1655

27. *The Betrothal of the Holy Virgin and St. Joseph* by James Tissot, c. 1894

28. *Rebecca Meets Isaac by the Way* by James Tissot, c. 1902

29. *Jewish Wedding in Morocco* by Eugene Delacroix, c. 1863

30. *Jewish Festivals*, ldsperspectives.com/

31. *The Matchmaker* by Gerard van Honthorst, c. 1625

32. *The Four Cups*, Jennifer Rigsby, Photographer, 2012

33. *Israel in Egypt* by Sir Edward John Poynter, c. 1867

34. *The Signs on the Door* by James Tissot, c. 1896

35. *The Exodus Panorama* by James Tissot, c. 1896-1902

36. *The Jews' Passover* by James Tissot, c. 1896

37. *The Last Supper* in stained glass by Charles Fairfax Murray, Christ Church, Oxford, England

38. *The Last Supper* by James Tissot, c. 1890

39. *Communion of the Apostles* aka *The Institution of the Eucharist* by Joos van Wassenhove, c. 1470

40. *The Palm Sunday Procession on the Mount of Olives* by James Tissot, c. 1896-1894

41. *The Ancient Ruins at Capernaum*, Author's Archive

42. *The Healing of Malcus* by James Tissot, c. 1896

43. *The Wine Mixed with Myrrh* by James Tissot, c. 1886-94

44. *The Crucifixion* by Simon Vouet, c. 1622

45. *The Rending of the Veil* by William Bell Scott, c. 1868

THE HOUSE OF STEPHANAS

2288 Gunbarrel Road, Suite 154-148
Chattanooga, TN 37421

The House of Stephanas is a non-profit humanitarian organization founded in 2005 by Dr. Richard (Rick) Sharp. To satisfy his quest to become a world-changer he raised support and assisted in a variety of ministries around the world, particularly those within the state of Israel. Rick followed the example of the house of Stephanas:

> *Let all your things be done with charity. I beseech you, brethren, (ye know the house of Stephanas, that it is the firstfruits of Achaia, and that they have addicted themselves to the ministry of the saints,) That ye submit yourselves unto such, and to every one that helpeth with us, and laboureth.*
>
> 1 Corinthians 16:14-16 KJV

> *Go ye therefore, and teach all nations, baptizing them in the name of the Father, and of the Son, and of the Holy Ghost: Teaching them to observe all things whatsoever I have commanded you: and, lo, I am with you alway, even unto the end of the world. Amen.*
>
> Matthew 28:19-20 KJV

To support Rick's legacy of global ministry, purchase books, audio recording or download of Dr. Sharp's teaching on *The Four Cups of Betrothal* contact The House of Stephanas:

4TheHOS@gmail.com

Visit our Facebook page: *The House of Stephanas*

CPSIA information can be obtained
at www.ICGtesting.com
Printed in the USA
JSHW040512241020
9042JS00003B/10